REINCARNATION

WHEELS OF A SOUL

Rabbi Berg, the world's foremost authority on the Kabbalah, sets a course that is both thought-provoking and most fascinating in knowing your *real* self.

If you have started your journey into the most awesome adventure a man or woman can undertake — birth, rebirth and adventure — *Wheels of a Soul* is recommended equipment for the first step.

With a sound, authoritative approach Rabbi Berg offers a *wealth* of information on one of the most controversial subjects of modern man, the daring truth of reincarnation.

An impressive, revolutionary new view of the nature of man, a most useful book that may well affect *your* life today — and tomorrow.

In *Wheels of a Soul*, Rabbi Berg takes us on a mind-boggling, interdisciplinary voyage of a cosmic soul, a saga still being written, as science continues to revolutionize our understanding of the origin, evolution, and destiny of mankind all that lies on the edge of infinity.

A living Kabbalist and the rarest of teachers, Rabbi Berg presents in this exciting and elegantly written book, a new frame of reference in a field neglected by science and too often misinterpreted by practicing psychiatrists and psychologists.

KABBALAH CENTRE BOOKS

*The Zohar 24 volumes by Rabbi Shimon bar Yohai, The cardinal work in the
literature of Kabbalah. Original Aramaic text with Hebrew translation and commentary
by Rabbi Yehudah Ashlag*

Miracles, Mysteries, and Prayer Volumes I,II, Rabbi Berg (also available in Spanish and Russian)

Kabbalah for the Layman Volume I, Rabbi Berg (also available in Hebrew, Spanish,
French, Russian, Italian, German, Persian, Chinese and Portuguese)

Kabbalah for the Layman Volumes II, III, Rabbi Berg (also available in Hebrew, Spanish,
French and Italian)

Astrology: The Star Connection, The Science of Judaic Astrology Rabbi Berg (also available
in Hebrew, Spanish, French and Persian)

Time Zones: Creating Order from Chaos Rabbi Berg (also available in French, Spanish,
Hebrew and Persian)

To The Power of One Rabbi Berg (also available in French and Spanish)

Power of the Aleph Beth Volumes I, II, Rabbi Berg (also available in Hebrew, French and Spanish)

The Kabbalah Connection Rabbi Berg (also available in Spanish and Hebrew)

Kabbalistik Astrology Made Easy Rabbi Berg in French Translation

Gift of the Bible Rabbi Yehudah Ashlag, Foreword by Rabbi Berg (also available in French,
Hebrew and Spanish)

Zohar: Parashat Pinhas Volumes I, II, III, Translated , compiled and edited by Rabbi Berg
(also available in Spanish)

An Entrance to the Tree of Life Rabbi Yehudah Ashlag, Compiled and edited by Rabbi Berg
(also available in Spanish)

Ten Luminous Emanations Rabbi Yehudah Ashlag, Volumes I, II, Compiled and edited by
Rabbi Berg (also available in Hebrew , 7 Volume set)

An Entrance to The Zohar Rabbi Yehudah Ashlag, Compiled and edited by Rabbi Berg

General Principles of Kabbalah Rabbi M. Luzzatto (also available in Italian)

Light of Redemption by Rabbi Levi Krakovsky

Kabbalistik Children's Stories:

Heaven on Your Head, Tales of the Enlightened, Legends of Israel, Legends of Zion
DR. S. Z. Kahana

SOON TO BE PUBLISHED

Secret Codes of the Universe Rabbi Berg

Kabbalistik Astrology Made Easy Rabbi Berg

Ten Luminous Emanations Volumes III, IV, Rabbi Yehudah Ashlag , compiled and edited by Rabbi Berg

Miracles, Mysteries, and Prayer Volume I, II, Rabbi Berg, in French Translation

Time Zones: Creating Order from Chaos Rabbi Berg, in Russian Translation

To The Power of One Rabbi Berg, in Russian Translation

Gift of the Bible Rabbi Yehudah Ashlag, Foreword by Rabbi Berg, in Russian Translation

BOOKS AND TAPES AVAILABLE
AT BOOKSELLERS AND KABBALAH CENTRES AROUND THE WORLD

WHEELS
OF A
SOUL

WHEELS OF A SOUL

REINCARNATION
YOUR LIFE
TODAY AND TOMORROW

RABBI BERG

Library of Congress Cataloging in Publication data

Rabbi Berg
Wheels of a Soul
Includes Bibliographical references and index.

1. Reincarnation

First Printing - June 1984
Second Printing - October 1985
Third Printing - February 1987
Fourth Printing - February 1989

REVISED EDITION
First Printing - December 1991
Second Printing - July 1995

0-943688-13-2 (Soft Cover)

COVER PHOTOGRAPH: LENNART NILSSON, A CHILD IS COMING, DELL PUBLISHING CO., 1990
COVER DESIGN: DIANNE EASTMAN/PIPPA WHITE

For further information:

THE KABBALAH LEARNING CENTRE
83-84 115th Street, Richmond Hill
NEW YORK, 11418
Tel. (718) 805-9122

— or —

P.O. BOX 14168
THE OLD CITY, JERUSALEM

PRINTED IN U.S.A.
1995

"Observe that all spirits are compounded of male and female, and when they go forth into the world ... the two elements are separated. If a man is worthy they are afterwards united, and it is then that he truly meets his mate and there is a perfect union both in spirit and flesh ..."

Zohar, Vol. 11, Ki Tazria

This book is dedicated by

Malkah Ḥanna
bat Israel and Ḥaya Sura Faigel

Thank you,

HaRav and Karen,

for the opportunity you are giving me to share the wisdom of Kabbalah and its Light. May the merit of this book unite all soulmates to bring Mashiah in our time. Amen

Kol Tov,

Melissa Anne Orenstein

"בא וראה כל הרוחות בעולם כלולים מזכר ונקבה, וכשיוצאאים לעולם הזה, יוצאים זכר ונקבה, ואח"כ מתחלקים כפי דרכם... ואח"כ, אם האדם זוכה, מזדווגים יחד. והיינו בת זוגו, ומתחברים בזווג אחד, בכל, ברוח ובגוף"

זהר, כרך יא׳ פרשת תזריע

ספר זה מוקדש על ידי

מלכה חנה
בת ישראל וחיה שרה פייגל

תודה

לרב ולקרן

שנתנו לי את ההזדמנות ואת ההדרכה
לחלק את חכמת הקבלה, ובזכות ספר זה
יתאחדו כל הזוגות בעולם, ואחדות
זו תביא לביאת המשיח במהרה בימינו, אמן.

כל טוב

ממליסה אן אורנשטיין

For my wife,
Karen,
In the vastness of cosmic space
and infinity of lifetimes,
it is my bliss
to share with you,
my soulmate,
the Age of Aquarius.

About the Centres

Kabbalah is mystical Judaism. It is the deepest and most hidden meaning of the Torah, or Bible. Through the ultimate knowledge and mystical practices of Kabbalah one can reach the highest spiritual levels attainable. Many people rely on belief, faith and dogma in pursuing the meaning of life, the unknown and the unseen. Yet, Kabbalists seek a spiritual connection with the Creator and the forces of the Creator. The strange thus becomes familiar, and faith becomes knowledge.

Throughout history, those who knew and practiced the Kabbalah were extremely careful in their dissemination of the knowledge — for they knew the masses of mankind had not yet been prepared for the ultimate truth of existence. Today Kabbalists know that it is not only proper, but necessary, to make the Kabbalah available to all who seek it.

The Kabbalah Learning Centre is an independent, non-profit institute founded in Israel in 1922. The Centre provides research, information and assistance to those who seek the insights of Kabbalah. The Centre offers public lectures, classes, seminars and excursions to mystical sites at branches in Israel — in Jerusalem, Tel Aviv, Haifa, Beer Sheva — and in the United States in New York and Los Angeles. Branches have been opened in Mexico, Toronto, Florida, North Miami, Paris, and London. Thousands of people have benefited by the Centre's activities. The publication of its Kabbalistic material continues to be the most comprehensive of its kind in the world. It includes translations in English, Hebrew, Russian, German, Portuguese, French, Spanish, Farsi (Persian) and Chinese.

Kabbalah can provide true meaning in one's being and the knowledge necessary for one's ultimate benefit. It can point towards a spirituality beyond belief. The Research Centre of Kabbalah will continue to make the Kabbalah available to all those who seek it.

ABOUT THE AUTHOR

RABBI BERG is Dean of the Research Centre of Kabbalah. Born in New York City, into a family descended from a long line of Rabbis, he is an ordained Orthodox Rabbi (from the renowned rabbinical seminary Torat VaDaat). While traveling to Israel in 1962, he met his Kabbalistic master, Rabbi Yehuda Zvi Brandwein, student of Rabbi Yehuda Ashlag Z"L and then Dean of the Research Centre of Kabbalah. During that period the Centre expanded substantially with the establishment of the United States branch in 1965 through which it currently disseminates and distributes its publications. Rabbi Berg did research at the Centre under the auspices of his beloved teacher Rabbi Brandwein Z"L, writing books on such topics as the origins of Kabbalah, creation, cosmic consciousness, energy, and the myths of the speed of light and the light barrier. Following the death of his master in 1969, Rabbi Berg assumed the position of Dean of the Centre, expanding its publication program through the translation of source material on the Kabbalah into English and other languages. Rabbi Berg moved with his devoted and dedicated wife Karen to Israel in 1971, where they opened the doors of the Centre to all seekers of self identity, establishing centres in all major cities throughout Israel, while at the same time lecturing at the City University of Tel Aviv. They returned to the United States in 1981 to further establish centres of learning in major cities all over the world. In addition to publishing scientific and popular articles, Rabbi Berg is the author, translator and/or editor of eighteen other books, including the Kabbalah for the Layman series, Time Zones and To the Power of One.

ACKNOWLEDGEMENTS

My greatest debt for the writing of Wheels of a Soul is owed to Kenneth R. Clark, editor at United Press International for compiling, reviewing and editing the manuscript, and for his writing a preface to this book. He made fundamental and frequent contributions to the essential ideas and their connections to the overall style. The delight I found in our many discussions is one of my principal rewards from this book.

Many thanks to Roy Tarlow for his helpful suggestions and proofreading of the manuscript. I would also like to thank Holly Clark for transcribing many of the tapes of lectures I had given on reincarnation. A special note of thanks to Navah Yardeni for her selfless assistance in the preparation of part of the manuscript.

TABLE OF CONTENTS

love-making

Chapter 10: Soulmates 73

Male and female; Two halves of one soul; Karmic debt of the male; Tikune of the female; Marriage

Chapter 11: Reincarnation and Evil 75

Misery and injustice; Souls laden with evil; Heredity; Differences in human beings; Free will

Chapter 12: The Man who Returned as his Nephew 77

Perceived enemy of religion; The human jigsaw puzzle; Immortal human soul; Metaphysical genetic code; Biblical name; Accidental murder; Metaphysical DNA; Predetermination; Prior intelligence; Framework of the metaphysical DNA; Environmental and biological process; Suicide

Chapter 13: Recalling Past Lives 83

No disappearance; Accessing the data; Hypnotism; Regression; Bridie Murphy; Astral body; Meditation; Cosmic consciousness; The tunnel; Out-of-body experience; Fears and phobia; Aleviation of fear

Chapter 14. Breaking the Code 89

The Hebrew letters; The transfer of energy; Memory; Useless guilt; Family hatreds

PART FOUR
THE EXPRESSION OF REINCARNATION

PART FIVE
UNIVERSAL REINCARNATION

inadvisable; Male and female; Incarnation of male soul into woman; Spiritual children; Sperm and egg; Divorce; Freedom of will and power of choice; Former lifetimes; Natal frequency, restriction and DNA; First and second husbands; A miniature star war

Marriage and how can I be sure; Planning the wedding; David and Bath-Sheba; Divorce as a precept; A marriage made in heaven; Prevention of a death sentence; Obstacles to soulmate marriages; Second marriage

Finding the key; The charts; An interface of our essence; Unity between man and universe; Sun signs; Lunar-Solar system; Cleansing of the soul; Cosmic clues; Choosing a lifetime partner

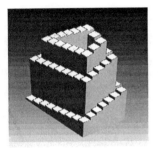

PREFACE

THIS BOOK IS ABOUT BIRTH, REBIRTH AND ADVENTURE — the mightiest and most awesome adventure a man or a woman can undertake. It is an odyssey that spans not years, but multiple lifetimes, carrying the individual through centuries of love, strife, pain, joy and the inevitable acquisition and discharge of the cosmic debt by which the soul ultimately is weighed.

This book, in short, is about reincarnation: how it happens, why it happens and where it leads in the cosmos of Kabbalah — a universe viewed in centuries past by a comparative handful of Jewish scholars pledged more to the concealment of its power than to dissemination of its wisdom. Much has been written in recent years about reincarnation but little of it has been valid simply because the authors have not had access to Kabbalah, the ancient body of Jewish mystic wisdom in which an understanding of reincarnation — be it Eastern or Western in concept — is rooted. Now, for reasons that will unfold in their own time, that wisdom has become available to all — Jews and non-Jews alike — who desire to receive it. It is to that desire and its fulfillment that this book is dedicated.

KENNETH R. CLARK
United Press International

INTRODUCTION

NEARLY 20 YEARS HAVE PASSED SINCE I MET MY MASTER, Rabbi Brandwein, and set out to learn the path of Kabbalah so that eventually I might lead others along its way. To my dismay, however, research on the delicate and vital subject of reincarnation and the importance of its place in Kabbalah soon revealed just how little knowledge of the subject was available to the general public.

To my great disappointment, when I first began to delve into the subject of reincarnation I found very little that had been written by contemporary Jewish Kabbalists. Most of the work that has been done on this subject has been that of non-Jewish scholars. I soon learned that when the subject of reincarnation came up among Jews, I found a non-interest and a latent denial that reincarnation had ever related to or had any connection with Judaism.

It is certainly not to the credit of Jewish scholarship that the works of a few writers — the Zohar itself, and the Ari and his volume, "*The Gates of Reincarnation*" — who were really informed on the subject have never really been taken seriously and certainly no interpretation or attempt to understand their works has ever been recorded.

Even as I sought to amass data on reincarnation through discussion with other Jewish scholars, I encountered bitter antagonism. Their feelings were that since the authorized guardians of the Kabbalah have never written on reincarnation in any great detail, but that non-Jewish scholars have, the whole subject is best left alone.

It is the supreme irony that Kabbalah, as ancient and as Jewish as Judaism itself, should wither in its home garden only to flourish among Christians, few of whom are aware of the true origin of the mysteries of their faith. Apart from its basis in the Bible, the inner essence of Christianity is wholly Kabbalistic. There is even a form of Kabbalah in Islam. These devotees of wisdom are not chary of dispensing it, but for all the secretiveness of the past among Jewish Kabbalists, mere covetousness — itself a Kabbalistic anathema — is not sufficient to explain why Jews have not written and publicly taught more.

Much of the reason for keeping details of Kabbalah under wraps has been that until the present age there was simply no viable way to teach it. Only when knowledge of electricity, basic physics and even the general principles of quantum mechanics were in possession of the average person could Kabbalah be taught in any span of time shorter than a lifetime.

Kabbalah, which is as far removed from religion as are chemistry or physics, has always drawn hostile fire from both religionists and scientists. The religionists feared the "blasphemy" of its logic and the scientists feared the metaphysics that took it beyond the scientific scope of the day. Only with the coming of Einstein with his theory of relativity and examination of the sub-atomic world could the gap between scientist and Kabbalist be bridged. And only with the coming of the Age of Aquarius — the Messianic era — could the gap between religionist and Kabbalist find its span. Now, for the first time ever, the basic article of faith for Jew and Christian alike which is "Love Thy Neighbor" can be shown in a mathematical formula.

This first volume of Reincarnation will be more than just a brief outline of the subject's structure as revealed in some of the classics of Jewish mysticism. These ancient works are, unfortunately, obscure to the point of being opaque. Frequently, when I try to define and clarify the concept of reincarnation, I am drawn back to Rabbi Ashlag's interpretation of the Zohar. Merely to record what he wrote, however, would leave me with the question of who is going to explain Rabbi Ashlag's explanation? His explanation was indeed abstruse, and as a Kabbalist, I believe that, at the time of his writing, the time had not yet come to reveal the innermost secrets of reincarnation.

Now, however, all mankind is moving into the age of Aquarius — the Messianic era in which Jew and non-Jew alike must ultimately write the final chapter of their existence.[1] The secrets of Kabbalah and reincarnation alike must be revealed and I will attempt not only to summarize them here, but also to interpret them and give them meaning for layman and scholar alike.

In the process, this book will challenge several notions about the Kabbalah and the Jewish view of reincarnation which remain to be accepted. That challenge, and the correction that must follow it, is the great task of Jewish scholarship in our generation. It is a generation of general Diaspora (exile) — religious and social for Jew and Christian alike. It has seen dwindling numbers of Jews and a great shrinking of Christian church congregations throughout the world. I believe a growing lack of spirituality in both credos is to blame. Without the spirituality, people — more hungry than ever for spiritual illumination or simply acceptance as human beings — are turning to other sources for meaningful explanations of their own lives and the lives of family and friends. Unhappily, those to whom they turn frequently lack information or scholarship based on the truest and most comprehensively knowledgeable publications containing the bulk of information on reincarnation.

By that, of course, I refer to the Zohar and Rabbi Isaac Luria's "*Gates of Reincarnation*", both of which will be drawn upon extensively here.

The task of rewriting this material with an eye toward emphasizing a deeper understanding of the interplay of religious and social forces involved in the study of reincarnation will produce some ideas that initially may seem strange and foreign. Yet, if I am to be successful in making a serious contribution to this very important and much needed subject, they must be presented. I will attempt to present them as clearly and concisely as possible.

Any book on reincarnation must first pose and answer three questions: (I) What is reincarnation?; (2) Where can the case for reincarnation be found in the Bible?; (3) How can one recognize one's own reincarnation? In answering these questions, and the multitude of other questions they will inspire, I will not present anything new.

It is a curious fact that for all the doubt and misinformation extant on the subject of reincarnation, there are almost as many definitions of the term as there are writers on the subject. Very few of those writers are Jewish, yet it is in Judaism that the truth of the matter can be found.

To know the truth, we must go to the source and that source is the Bible. Ecclesiastes 1:4 states, "One generation passes away and another generation comes but the earth abides forever". The Zohar[2] tells us that what this verse really means is that the generation that has passed away is the same generation that comes to replace it. An identical key may be found in the Ten Commandments (Exodus 20:5) which says, "The sins of the fathers are remembered even unto the third and fourth genera-tion".[3] This does not imply, as some erroneously have contended, that God is so full of wrath that he is not content to punish merely the sinner, but that he will inflict punishment for sin upon the sinner's innocent grandchildren and great grandchildren as well. Who could rationally love and worship so fierce and vengeful a deity? The Zohar reveals that the truth of that verse is that the third and fourth generations are, in fact, the first — one soul returning in the form of its own descendants so that it may correct the sins cited as "sins of the fathers".[4]

Such examples in support of the case for reincarnation abound in the Bible and in the course of this book, we shall explore many of them. But the concept of reincarnation is by no means exclusive to Judaism. The idea was prevalent among Indians on the American continent; and in the Orient, the tea-ching of reincarnation is widespread and influential. It is the basis of most of the philosophical systems of India where hundreds of millions accept the truth of reincarnation the way we accept the truth of gravity — as a great natural and inevitable law that only a fool would question. Indeed, Jews are not the only ones with a need and a hunger to endure.

Obviously then, reincarnation is one of the fundamental religious ideas of mankind — almost equal to belief in the existence of God Himself. Yet most authors writing on the subject show no knowledge of the origin of the idea. The Zohar clearly states that origin and "*The Gates of Reincarnation*"[5] amplifies it. But like every idea of great antiquity, the concept of reincarnation has come to most of the world in a welter of superstition and misconception. Superstition is so repellant to the Western way of thinking, that great discredit has been cast on the philosophical value of the central idea of reincarnation itself. Who of us, after all, wishes to contemplate being reincarnated as a dog, or returning as a stone? Yet. beneath all the fancies there lurks a basic and eternal truth. How else could the idea have endured for so many thousands of years? How could it have attracted so many able thinkers?

One question asked since time immemorial — with even more emphasis since the horror of the Holocaust — is this: If God really exists, why is there so much misery in the world? Why is there so much undeserved suffering, so many unearned gifts and unpunished crimes? Why are strong men suddenly stricken blind, innocent children scourged with disease, nursing mothers killed by drunken fools speeding in automobiles? Must we assume that God doesn't care? Is He so powerless that He cannot change such conditions?

In this world, is right rewarded and wrong punished? It takes little observation to answer that question. All too often, the criminal goes free; the innocent is imprisoned and the mediocre one gains riches.

The Bible[6] tells us of a time to come in which our punishments will be recompensed and our sins forgiven. Down through the centuries, the Jew has longed for that world, and the

Zohar shows that the very longing, with eyes always turned toward the world to come, is what has made it possible for the Jew to endure.[7]

If God has really created a world as wretched as this one seems to be, what hope have we, in the name of logic, to expect something better in Heaven? If all souls are equal at birth, why are human destinies so unequal? Are we to fall back upon the hopeless doctrine of predestination and the elect? Why aren't we all given a chance to develop our powers? Is it all a matter of chance? Can we conceive of an ordered universe in which the working of human destiny is left to blind chance?

Is it not significant that all other workings of the universe are guided by natural laws and principles?

As far as this world is concerned, human equality is a myth! Despite the orations of politicians, we are unequal mentally, spiritually, and morally. Opportunity and limitations seem forever to be playing a game of tag with our plans. Some have strong, healthy bodies; others are frail and diseased. Some have quick and capricious brains; others are dull and limited.

Equality is denied by every fact of nature. The environment holds only inequality. One child, born in Africa, is restricted by that birth to a life of utmost narrowness. Another is born in the midst of an advanced civilization with every educational and cultural advantage. One is born in a foul, dark room in a tenement. Another is born in a home of refinement to be reared in the best of surroundings.

If there are souls and they are equal at birth, why should there be this favoritism? Is there no law or purpose in the assignment of the law in our respective destinies? One man may work hard all his life and at the very end of it wind up an in-patient in a dreary hospital or charity home. Another inherits a vast estate and draws upon the luxuries of the world as though they were his personal bank account, even though he may be an idler a parasite, a useless member of society. Why should this be so? It is not right to say it is a matter of intellect, for many bright men have failed and many fools have money springing from under their fingertips. Turn where we will, the world is full of stark inequalities and inexplicable contrasts.

The Bible[8] tells us that behind every event there is God; but we are not able to prove it by pointing to the condition of the world. On the contrary, moral chaos seems more in evidence than moral order. Is it any wonder, therefore, that Jews and Christians throughout the world have been leaving synagogues and churches in increasing numbers? Judaism and Christianity, in their present state, both are failing because we have become convinced that Adam never existed.

What is needed today is a master key to unlock the apparent chaos and find order within it. Reincarnation, stripped of superstition and half-truth, can be that key. The importance of this work is to present the vital truth of reincarnation.

It is astounding how quickly thoughtful people have come to regard it with favor. It is only in the past few years that people have begun to take reincarnation seriously, much less make it a working part of their lives. Today it is reasonable to say that millions of people in the Western world look upon reincarnation as the logical explanation of so many social, religious, humanistic and environmental problems. This acceptance has spread far beyond the limits of the original Kabbalah. Courses in the subject have been widely offered and just as widely accepted. Because their teachers have not been versed in

Kabbalah, most of such courses have captured only a fraction of the structure. Yet that which has been offered has become instrumental in the betterment of lives. Because the concept of reincarnation is a rational tool for dealing with the most baffling of human problems both in the Jewish and in the non-Jewish community, it is unequalled in its power to convince, illuminate and inspire.

Unhappily, few people ever take time out to explore just what their views may be as to the truth of what really troubles the world. If they did, they would be very surprised to discover just how much is taken for granted as truth without any real thought about the matter at all.

For example. when a child is born, we take for granted that its consciousness was created with its body that the internal aspect of the individual which we call a soul is there and that it is inevitable that it will be there as long as the child lives. Why do we accept the proposition that the internal element inside us determines our actions? In Kabbalah for the Layman,[9] it is shown why this is taken for granted with little thought beyond that which seems obvious.

Briefly stated, it is as follows: In a child, we see the apparent development of the consciousness — the mind and the growth of that mind with the passage of time. We see the growth of the mind parallel to the development of the body. In old age, the consciousness and awareness suddenly disappears with the death of the body. Therefore, it seems safe to assume that there was something internal that could not be perceived, but nevertheless had to exist. Some might argue that the brain produces consciousness and that much of what we believe to be internal has actually been produced by the physical brain. but this is by no means the only explanation.

The growth of a child in its early years is so phenomenal, given the short span of the child's existence, that we really can't say such development is purely at the physical level. When the instrument is destroyed and the consciousness can no longer make itself felt physically, is the annihilation of the mind and the soul implied? No!

The soul of a man is no more dependent upon the existence of the brain than a musician is dependent upon the existence of his violin though both instruments are necessary for musical expression in the physical world. Only when we can fully grasp this viewpoint can we begin to approach the study of reincarnation. Human consciousness existed before birth, and by human consciousness, I mean the soul. This is the first fundamental fact of reincarnation.

In the course of this work, I will attempt to make it quite obvious that death comes only for the body. The soul lives eternally. It is this missing element of understanding that has prevented us from taking a world view of ourselves, in an objective way, rather than merely watching events as they move across the stage of our lives and viewing them as unrelated parts of the scene that spans a scant 70 to 120 years.

My intention is not to prove that reincarnation is a fact of nature, although a preponderance of evidence supports such a proposition. Anyone who feels the need for strict scientific validation should realize that as we probe deeper into the subatomic world of our existence, we find that strict scientific validation of anything becomes virtually impossible. Quantum mechanics and the now scientifically respectable "Uncertainty Principle" have taken care of that. Essentially, verification lies not in accumulation of more stringent proofs of reincarnation, but rather in the persuasion of skeptics to accept that which has already been made known.

How do scientists really work? Observing the methodology implied in the selection of Nobel laureates, the advance of scientific knowledge is rarely a neat sequence from theoretical prediction to observational proof. It is rather the imagination, the sudden flash of insight that has produced the greatest advances within the scientific community. Science has never been an ingathering of known facts, nor has it ever been a set of subjects dealing with natural phenomena. Instead it is a way of discovering what our world is all about by venturing theories and then subjecting these theories to the test of observation and experiment. Between the abstract world of conjecture and the real world of experimentation there will always exist a continuous strain and sometimes even conflict. In essence, scientists of renown have rarely waited for questions to be raised. They have instead made new discoveries by extending their groping fingers far beyond their mental processes.

Having observed that many people's social condition makes it impossible for them to survey the evidence of survival of death with an unprejudiced eye, I believe a new approach can be taken. Just as it is impossible to convince a blind man that there are stars if he is already convinced that the sky is a solid black canopy, so it may seem impossible to break through the prejudices the very thought of reincarnation arouses in many. Yet if an operation could be performed to restore the blind man's sight, further debate would be unnecessary.

This book is offered then as an attempt to popularize an operative procedure that will enable people to open the eye of inner vision, and in so doing, to understand that man is a creature who can achieve a more exalted state of being.

As I have explained in *Kabbalah for the Layman*,[10] we are not dealing with a religious issue. Reincarnation is not a question of faith or doctrine, but of logic and reason. Yet, the Bible is its fountainhead. In this book I will present not only existing information but also, for the first time, new source material to demonstrate that reincarnation is very much a fact of life whatever the credo or doctrine under which that life is lived.

The multifaceted developments of reincarnation will provide for all men and women one of the central reasons for their existence. It will explain why we behave as we do.

Part One

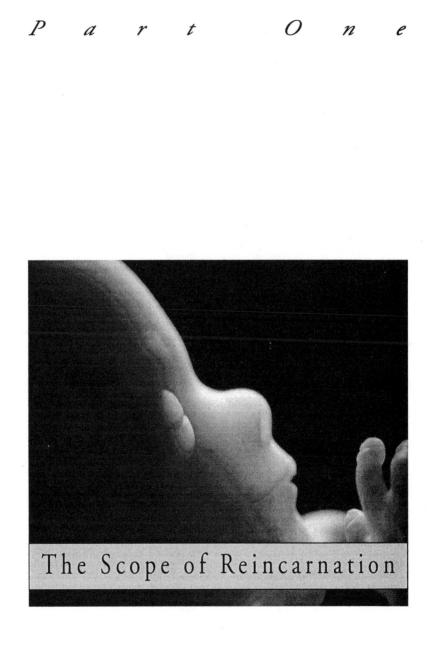

The Scope of Reincarnation

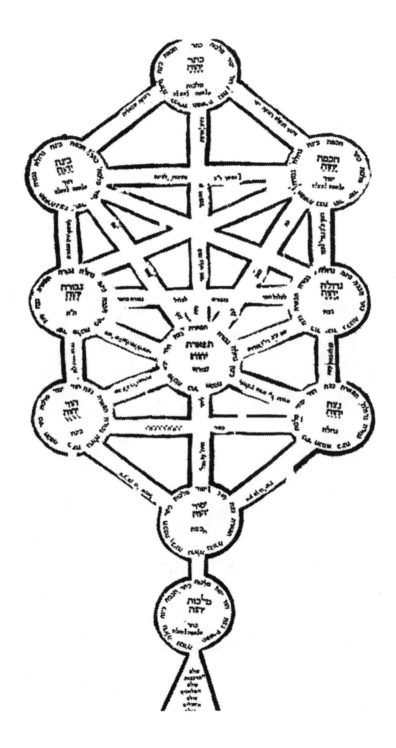

1

RELIGION AND SCIENCE

MANY OF US BELIEVE THAT BEYOND THE NEED TO SURVIVE, there is no explanation for human life. Others never give the matter so much as a thought, preferring to enjoy the pleasures of the moment. Yet all who have been raised in Jewish or other traditions have their own beliefs concerning human life and suffering and beliefs that every human has a soul and that soul is immortal.

Suffering, we believe, is a test given to us by God with heaven or hell the reward or the punishment that awaits us. We believe, not because we have proof, but because these things have been taught to us on the authority of our parents and prelates who picked it up from their parents and rabbis and religious teachers all the way back to the authority of the Bible.

Since the Renaissance, however, Western man has become increasingly skeptical of knowledge handed down on the strength of authority alone — be that authority a person or a book.

Skepticism is encouraged for all beliefs that cannot survive the relentless proof of the scientific laboratory.

Ptolemy said that the sun revolved around the earth. Later Copernicus developed the instrument that proved it was the other way around. Once it was almost the universal belief that the earth was flat. Then came Columbus, Magellan and other intrepid adventurers to overthrow the conviction by sailing west and arriving back home from the east. By these, and by hundreds of other demonstrations, man gradually came to see that the ancient authorities could be wrong. Discovery after discovery shattered and disarranged the neat and orderly picture which mankind had believed to be beyond challenge.

No one has ever been able to see or detect a soul. Immortality? Who ever came back to tell us about it? Heaven? Our telescopes show no evidence. God? The result, the learned say, of a mind that needs a father substitute.

The universe is a colossal machine and man is a little machine — both made possible by an arrangement of atoms in a natural evolutionary process. Suffering is man's inescapable struggle for survival — nothing more. Death is merely a dissolution of chemical elements. The "facts" are in — just as they were when the sun revolved around a flat earth.

Science was born of our own five senses. It has expanded our senses, to be sure, with microscopes, telescopes and radar. It has systematized our sense of observation with reasoning, mathematics and the technology of experimentation. But one thing remains. Science is still the testimony of our five senses.

Questions about the essential nature of things are answered in classical physics by the Newtonian model of the universe. The properties of the atom were first extracted from the macroscopic notion — of billiard balls, and thus from sensory experience. Whether or not the model could actually be applied to the world of the atom was never questioned. It was not even experimentally investigated until the 20th century when physicists were finally able to tackle the question of the ultimate nature of matter. With the aid of the most sophisticated technology the world had ever known, they were able to probe deeper and deeper into nature, uncovering one layer of matter after another. The existence of atoms was verified. Then the constituents of atoms were discovered — nuclei. electrons, and finally the components of the nuclei, the protons, neutrons and a host of other subatomic particles. As the complicated instruments of modern experimental physics penetrated the submicroscopic world into realms of nature far removed from our macroscopic environment, that world suddenly became accessible to our senses.

The subatomic world remains beyond our sensory perceptions, but with the help of modern instrumentation, we are able to observe the properties of atoms and their constituents in an indirect way. Yet we can only do so through a chain of processes ending in the audible click of a geiger counter or in a dark spot on a photographic plate. What we thus see and hear are never the investigated phenomena themselves, but always their consequences. Knowledge of matter at this level is no longer derived from direct sensory experience. Our language. therefore, which takes its images from the world of senses, is no longer adequate to describe the observed phenomena. As we probe deeper and deeper into nature, we must abandon more and more of the images and concepts of ordinary language.

On this journey to the world of the infinitely small, the most important step, from a philosophical point of view, was the first one taken. Once the physicist found himself dealing with the nonsensory experience of reality, he had to — unlike the capitalist — face the paradoxical aspect of experience. When Einstein developed his theory of relativity, he destroyed many of the fundamentals of physics by telling us that time is not invariable. With that, he opened the door to consideration of the validity of reincarnation.

The instruments we have created with our five senses, ironically, have turned to show us that this sensory equipment is itself imperfect and inadequate to acquaint us with the world as it really is. Radio waves, radioactivity and atomic energy are but a few of the phenomena that now show us to be surrounded by invisible waves and pulsations of energy. The most minute particles of matter contain forces of a magnitude so great that our imagination cannot encompass them.

If the scientist were to consider the very fundamental of fundamentals — the seed — he then would have to ask himself how this minute object can produce an infinite array of human beings with all of their diversities. The phenomenon of human sperm defies the imagination. The five senses could never adequately provide us with the tools by which the makings and workings of this seed are accomplished.

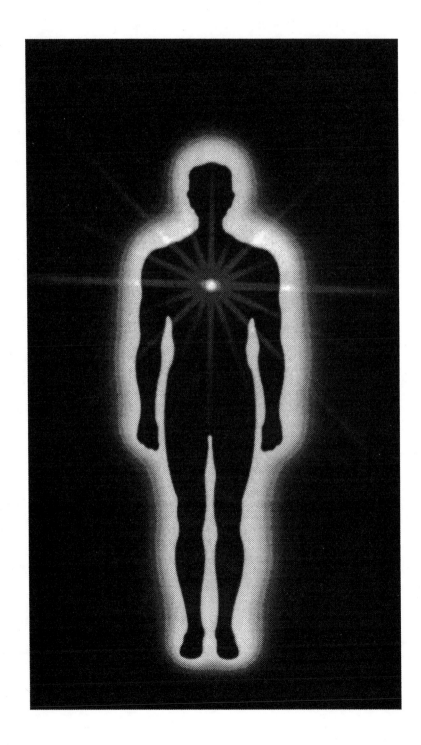

2

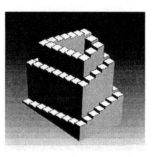

THE NEW AGE OF REALITY

WE ARE LOOKING AT THE WORLD THROUGH TINY PEEPHOLES — our eyes and our ears in the narrow sum of our bodies. Our vibratory sensitivity to light enables us to receive only a small fraction of the total light vibrations in existence. A 50-cent dog whistle will summon your dog, but you will not hear it because its vibratory frequency is above your uppermost limit of sensitivity.

There are many animals and insects whose range of seeing or hearing or smelling is different from our own. Consequently, their universe contains much that we cannot perceive. This is a curious spectacle — proud man, exceeded by animals, birds and even insects. A thinking man can only wonder about his perception of reality and hunger to view for himself some of these great invisibilities.

Suppose we were trained to use our sensory equipment in such a way that our vibratory sensitivity to light and sound were only slightly enlarged. Would we then not become aware of many objects that were, until then, undetectable by us? Suppose that a few of us were born with a slightly enlarged sensitivity range. Would that few then not see and hear things the rest of us do not see and hear? The often repressive history of man indicates a number of cases in which such enlarged sensitivities seem to have existed. Rabbi Shimon bar Yohai had awesome wisdom and power at his fingertips. Yet he and his son were forced to hide in a cave for years in order to reveal the Zohar.

But science has the capability of expanding man's sensitivities too, often into areas regarded as uncomfortably bizarre by other scientists. Semyon and Valentina Kirilian are an excellent example. In 1958, the two Soviet scientists, using a photographic technique known as early as the 1890's, captured on film for the first time an impression of the biological field that constitutes the human aura. The process, called electrophotography, also makes it possible to examine the pattern of luminescence around dozens of materials — rubber, coins, leaves, paper, textiles. The Kirilians found that the structural details of emanations were different for each item tested and photographed; but the most significant result of their penetrating study was the discovery that living things have patterns that are totally different from those emanated by inanimate objects. A metal coin is surrounded by a constant never-varying aura, but a living being gives a picture of myriad sparkling, shooting, flashing lights that glow like jewels.

In reporting results of their breakthrough, the scientists wrote: "What we saw in the panorama through the microscope and our optical instruments seemed like the control board of a huge computer. Here and there, lights brightened and dimmed, signals of processes inside. If something went wrong inside, or if conditions needed adjustment, the engineer at the control box could read the signals in the lights."

"In living things we see the signals of the inner state of the organism reflected in the brightness, dimness or color of the flares. The inner life of activities of a human being are written in these light hieroglyphs. We have created an apparatus to write these hieroglyphs, but to read them, we're going to need help".[11]

In "Behind the Iron Curtain", Oshtrand and Schroder, writing about the Kirilians, wrote, "The Kirilian team was working that evening on the photographs when something strange happened. From testing leaves from various plants, they knew that each species had its own unique energy pattern, like individual television set patterns broadcasting from each type of plant. But the photos of the twin leaves that the scientists had given them differed sharply from each other. Were the leaves from two different species of plants? Had they made an error? They did picture after picture with the same results."[12]

They could only confirm the individuality of each entity tested, however closely allied it might be to its own twin. Suddenly, in a world in which paranormal, metaphysical phenomena are seen to exist, and in which even the aura of an individual entity can prove to be different from even its twin, our five senses have become pathetic guides indeed.

3

THE DILEMMA OF UNEXPLAINED EVENTS

NO LONGER CAN WE DISMISS AS COINCIDENCE THE possibilities of unexplained events, and because of the great currents that sweep through our times, the task of alerting others to such events has become one of tremendous import and interest.

Few have known that better than Dr. J.D. Rhyne of Duke University. Since 1930, this far-sighted scientist and his associates have studied the telepathic and clairvoyant faculties of man. Under closely controlled experiments using scientific methods, Rhyne has discovered that many people exhibit evidence of extrasensory powers of perception under laboratory conditions. Careful statistical techniques have been used to evaluate Dr. Rhyne's experiments and, mathematically speaking, they have indicated that the results he has achieved could not possibly be attributed to chance.[13]

There is a growing body of evidence which is slowly undermining the traditional doubt of the Western world that powers of telepathic and clairvoyant nature exist in the human mental makeup. Laboratories have established clairvoyance as a possible mode of perception only. Its potential for usefulness has not even been scratched.

But that potential is enormous. Clearly if a man possesses a means of cognition that does not depend on his five senses — if he can, under certain conditions, see as though upon a television screen that which is happening elsewhere in space, without benefit of his physical eyes — then that man possesses an important tool for obtaining knowledge about himself and the universe.

Man has achieved great things through the centuries, but all his strength and flexibility, he remains fragile and vulnerable. For all his conquests, he is still impotent and bewildered. For all his art and culture, he still finds himself wondering about his suffering and the suffering of the ones dear to him from birth until death. Of late, however, he has penetrated the inner recesses of the atom and now, with his newly discovered faculties of extrasensory perception and his new recognition of the strained relationship between the conscious and the subconscious mind, he is on the brink of penetrating to the inner recesses of himself. Perhaps at long last he can find satisfying answers to the basic riddles of his existence. Perhaps now he will be able to understand the reasons for his birth and his pain and learn where it all leads other than to death.

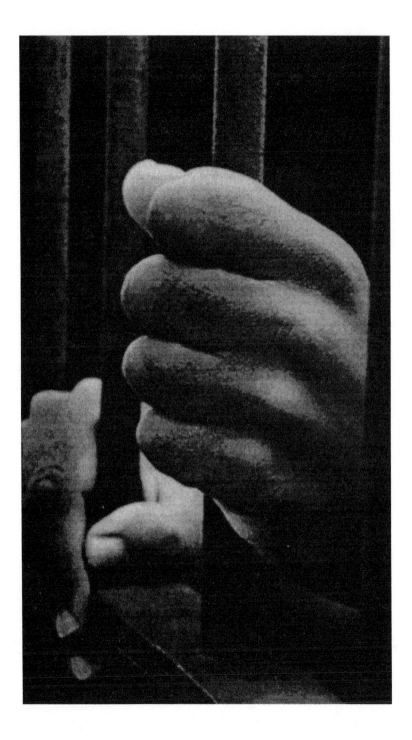

4

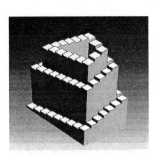

REINCARNATION AND HUMAN SUFFERING

IF GOD IS GOOD, LOVING, MERCIFUL AND JUST, WHY DO SO many millions of innocent people suffer while the guilty prosper and go free?

The question is almost as old as humankind itself. The answer is precisely as old, but only through the analogy of the wheel can it be grasped.

The Hebrew word for reincarnation is *Gilgul Neshamot* which means, literally, "wheel of the soul". It is to that vast metaphysical wheel with souls studding its rim like stars on the edge of a galaxy, that we must look if we are to see beyond the appearance of innocence punished and evil rewarded. *Gilgul Neshamot* is a wheel constantly in motion, and with its turning, souls come and go again and again in the cycle of birth, evolution, death and birth again. The same evolution occurs with the body in the course of a single lifetime. There is birth, cell growth, parenthood and death — new bodies produced by the old, thus giving rise to continuity of physical form. It is always a father imparting his seed for the sake of continuity, a never-ending process.

Understanding that process at the physical level is the key to just what a truthful view of continuum really means. Most who really consider it will be surprised to learn how much is taken for truth without any real thought about it at all. The whole tendency of physical evolution ranges from the simple to the complex. At one end of the organic series is the single cell, without organ or structure, and at the other end is the extraordinarily complex body with its millions of cells organized into organs, tissues and great networks of nerves and brain tissue. Our bodies constantly go through this evolution. The average school child is familiar with the process of protein and tissue passing through the process of birth, existence and decay. The brain of a baby has little power of response, but as the child grows, his mind becomes more in evidence — not so much because of the growth of the child, but because of a steady improvement in the instrument called consciousness. In old age, the brain becomes less responsive and the physical expression is dimmed. At death, the instrument is destroyed and the consciousness no longer can make itself felt physically. But that does not imply annihilation of the soul or even the mind. Ongoing evolution is central to the concept of reincarnation.

One of the great paradoxes of what we view as reality is the fact that while we recognize the universal inevitability of death, there is fear of dying. Physical bodies are sacrificed in war to keep other physical bodies alive. War is the result of man's endeavor to improve his lifestyle, but experience has always shown us that any such improvement is at someone else's expense. Mineral forms are broken apart to furnish food for plants, plants are sacrificed for animals and animals are sacrificed for man. From a physical point of view, nature is little more than a charnel house. Consequently, since nature patently cares so little for physical bodies, it is easy to wonder if anything has any purpose.

Still, it is equally observable that something in our universe keeps the continuum going. Growth, like the wheel, has no beginning and no end. But to view life merely as a beginning and an end is like viewing a tree in a forest and saying there is only the tree. The problem is born of the fact that we are lost in this continuum of time and motion. Everything in life, without exception, operates as a wheel from which it is impossible to look beyond the moment and see that in coming to earth many times, we gather experience and pass from one grade to another, even as we did in growing up as children. Even in the past we created primitive societies that evolved and graduated from a root civilization to what might be called a moral civilization. What we have reaped, for good or evil, is a continuous progression of experiences which can only be seen as incarnation following incarnation. We grow continually from agrarian societies to cities, from war to peace, and to war again, never really seeing beyond our place on the rim. We blindly accept the motion of the wheel that constitutes our lives without ever questioning to what end it turns. But a new age has dawned and all that is about to change.

Now that we have begun the Age of Aquarius, all who live can learn of Kabbalah. Because of the increase in light brought down by the sages of the past, we are moving from darkness to a new awareness of an ongoing movement in cosmology. We are capable, if we choose, of grasping the concept of the soul undergoing the revolving process without being limited by time to any particular body.

In my book, *Ten Luminous Emanations*, Vol II,[14] I describe in detail the difference between the generations. I do not wish to repeat it here, but as the Age of Aquarius is the Age of Enlightenment, it may be possible for even the skeptical to understand that knowledge we have acquired in past lives is with us today. We might even dare to say that people who learned such things in the past have returned through the continuum to this life with knowledge and experience to share with this era.

To do so requires a new and better set of eyes. The four seasons, viewed through the old ones, show little change. Isn't life really the same as it was last year? Are the seasons not still in the same order according to the same plan? Those who fail, either through fear or ignorance, to grasp the possibilities of reincarnation overlook the principle of the wheel that exists in every life form on earth.

This brings us back to the frustrating inequity of human suffering. The most common sources of such suffering are disease and old age. For all our scientific advancement, we have not even scratched the surface in the fight against these two villains. Nor do we profess any progress in solving the riddle of death itself. Fire, flood, disease and disaster are only the outer threats to peace, happiness and life. Inwardly the battle rages on against selfishness, stupidity, frivolity, hypocrisy and greed — all endless sources of pain. Moments of despair are interspersed with flights of fancy, high elation and the enduring hope that at the center of it all lies a heaven of love, beauty and understanding. The wheel turns on, leaving us to struggle in the mire of confusion, forever wondering about purpose — Who am I? Why am I here? Until these most basic questions of existence are answered, nothing is answered. Until reasons for pain have been explained, nothing has been explained. Until the suffering of the most insignificant creature has been accounted for, nothing has been accounted for and our philosophical grasp of life is incomplete.

5

REINCARNATION AND THE BIBLE

WE ARE TAUGHT FROM CHILDHOOD THAT IF WE DO something good, God will reward us and if we do something bad, He punishes us. It is as if God were standing somewhere above us like a stern parent saying, "Oh, you're good? Here's a piece of candy", or, "Oh, you're bad? Over the knuckles!" Never believe it. Such a simplistic view does no credit to the Creator and even less to His creation.

Most of us — Jew or Christian — have been raised with the concept of a soul which resides somewhere in the interior of our being and is immortal. We have been taught that suffering is essentially a test given to us by God and that heaven or hell will be the reward or the punishment that awaits us when life is over.

Reward and punishment are no different from the existence in your living room of an electrical socket. Screw a light-bulb into it and you will have the blessing of light. Stick your finger into it and you will receive a nasty shock. The results are neither reward nor punishment but merely the consequence of an individual's action in exercise of free will.

Still, millions cling to this scenario of reward and punishment, not because they have proof, but because they think the Bible spells it out. It is for the same reason that millions — Jew and non-Jew alike — refuse even to consider the possibility of reincarnation.

Where, they might say, is reincarnation mentioned in the authority we all hold so highly? The Book of Exodus[15] provides the full explanation, not only of reincarnation, but also of its effect in terms of parents and children, brothers and sisters and how all interrelate in the immediate environment.

These truths, however, depend upon our ability to remember our past lives. One of the strongest arguments against reincarnation lies in the question, "If we were born before, why don't we remember, and even if we did live before, why are we being punished now for things we can't even remember doing in some existence long ago?"

In Exodus,[16] the Lord forbids the making of pagan gods and commands, "Thou shalt not bow down unto them nor serve them. For I, the Lord thy God, am a jealous God, visiting the iniquities of the fathers upon the children unto the third and fourth generation of them that hate me." This particular verse has been the subject of many commentaries and much criticism, the argument, of course, being the injustice of punishing succeeding generations for the sins of one man or woman.

The laws of heredity, only now beginning to be thoroughly understood through DNA research, might seem to support the literal Biblical view of parental sin being passed along to offspring. If the short term greed that has produced chemical and radiation pollution of air and water supplies and indiscriminate use of drugs and various pharmacological remedies with little thought to side affects upon a developing fetus are "sins", then those sins certainly are passed along to the children — often several generations down the line — in the form of birth defects, congenital disease and mental retardation. There is, however, one apparent paradox in human development which heredity fails to explain. In the lower animal kingdom, little difficulty is encountered in attempting to formulate a system of scientific hereditary law. Kittens are virtual carbon copies of cats. Baby birds need no flying lessons once their feathers have developed. Man alone is different. The often vast divergence in mental and moral values between parents and their children would seem to go well beyond any blueprint found to date in DNA.

The verse about "Sins of the Fathers" does not mean what it seems to mean. Rather it has deeper significance. What it really indicates is that a given individual, sent into this world for the purpose of correction, fails to complete that correction and must return. The Bible never meant to imply that an innocent one would pay for sins committed by his father, but rather that the individual who has committed the sins literally is the father, returned in the third or fourth generation to pick up the task of correction where he left it. In a very literal sense of the word, he becomes his own great or great-great grandchild.

The Ari[17] says that the number of times this cycle must be repeated before correction is achieved depends upon the individual soul. If that soul lives one lifetime with no progress, it is allowed to return three more times at the maximum, and total failure will then result in that soul's reversion to the abyss.

In the literal translation of Exodus, the word generation is not mentioned. With that deletion, the meaning becomes clear. A man or woman may return three more times, for a total of four lives. If progress is made in any of those incarnations, then no further limit is imposed upon the number of reincarnations needed to complete the mission of correction. But even if progress is made, the danger of plunging backward in any lifetime is always present.

6

INCARNATION AT LOWER LEVELS

OF ALL WHO ACCEPT THE DOCTRINE OF REINCARNATION, Kabbalists alone, perhaps, believe that a soul can return at a lower level than the one it left in a previous life.[18] Indeed, if the weight of *tikune* (correction) is sufficiently heavy, a human soul may find itself reincarnated into the body of an animal, a plant, or even a stone.[19] Incredible as that statement may seem, it will explain many mysteries that have confronted and confounded man from his earliest beginnings to the peak of his science. It will throw light upon the subject of so called "hauntings", it will explain much that psychiatrists vainly attempt to explain about "mental illness".

It may even clarify the origin of one of the most ancient of myths — the tale in "A Thousand and One Nights" of the genie in the bottle.[20]

As a people, we are so quick to scoff at that which our five senses cannot detect or at that which the religious doctrine of our rearing has either denied or ignored. But what is a more metaphysically logical fate for the soul of a mass-murderer, for example, than to be locked in a stone?

For the soul to whom murder has become a way of life, reincarnation into a human body is not likely to result in anything beyond more murder, since the act of taking lives is the very manifestation of the individual's desire to receive.[21] From a Kabbalistic standpoint, it is possible that such a soul may return to this plane of time, space and motion as an inanimate object in which the Desire to Receive is a bare minimum. In such a hell of total confinement, a soul would be able to shed the *klipot* — the evil husks of negative energy — that have covered it, free of the awful ability to yield to the temptation to kill.

Not all who fall under the weight of their crimes, however, find themselves locked in stone. Depending upon the weight of the *klipot* which their negative energy has manufactured, they may return as animals or plants, and in so doing, leave vivid traces of the fact in what the medical profession calls "mental illness" or in what folklore may call "hauntings".

It is in the winter months especially, when the days are short and darkness rules, that tales of sounds emanating from seemingly inanimate objects or of stark and leafless trees that seem to brood with malevolent intelligence invade the consciousness. Take these as fairy tales or study them as legitimate metaphysical manifestations and it will be of little consequence, but do not think lightly of *ubar* —souls that may attach themselves to the unwary through consumption of the very animal or vegetable matter into which they have been incarnated.

Recent history abounds with stories of perfectly rational, even kind, people who, for no apparent reason, suddenly have become implacable and merciless killers; The Charles Whitman who climbed the tower at the University of Texas to rain death on the campus below with a high-powered rifle was not the Charles Whitman known on that campus as a shy and gentle student.

I know a woman who has been locked away in a psychiatric ward twice because she felt she was being bombarded by evil spirits and I can testify that she is as normal as any who are deemed mentally fit. That definition, in itself, is suspect. I believe that between 70 and 80 percent of all who live display "abnormal behavior" at one time or another and that in most of those cases an invading spirit of evil is the cause. Rites of exorcism might heal far more of the "mentally ill" than all of the drugs and electro-shock therapy employed by the psychiatric community. Psychiatrists, unhappily, are treating symptoms, with no knowledge of cause.

There is a tale[22] told of Shmuel Vital, the son of Haim Vital, that illustrates the point. He was in Egypt when a young woman was stricken mute and paralyzed two months after her marriage. Vital was summoned and because of the sudden onset of the affliction, he suspected possession by an evil spirit that somehow had managed to invade her being.

In the course of his examination, a male voice emanated from her — the soul of a man who told Vital he had loved her and was consumed with jealousy when she married another. He therefore had possessed her and rendered her unable to function as a wife to his rival. An exorcist was summoned and the text tells us he was able to draw out the possessing spirit and enclose it in a bottle which then was buried in the sand. — Note the parallel with an ancient rite detailed in the "Arabian Nights" of the story of the genie trapped in the bottle.

Had the unfortunate girl rescued from her spiritual bondage through the intercession of Shmuel Vital lived today, her fate probably would have been life in a psychiatric ward.

By now it should be quite clear that reincarnation is discussed and accepted in the Bible, and that by virtue of that acceptance it is an integral part of Judaism and Christianity alike.

A further clarification may be found in the Bible[23] which states, "Now these are the ordinances which thou shalt set before them.. should man acquire a Hebrew slave..." What follows would seem, upon casual reading, to be little more than a codification of rules governing the ownership and treatment of slaves— ordinances now irrelevant since the institution of slavery, at least in its formal sense, has been abolished in virtually every nation on earth. But "slaves", in the case of the verse cited, are only figures of speech — vessels to contain and thus reveal the means by which souls return into this world again.[24] The slavery in question is but every human's slavery to body energy. Another book would be needed to spell out all the specifics of the Exodus passage, but they are detailed in the Zohar. In a nutshell it means simply that each soul will be judged according to the sin that has been committed in a prior lifetime and incarnations will continue until all of those sins are corrected.

7

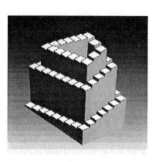

THE MATH CONNECTION

ONE PRIMARY OBJECTION VOICED BY SKEPTICS TOWARD THE concept of reincarnation is mathematical in nature. If the number of souls is finite and they keep returning through reincarnation, how can there be an increase in population?

The Bible[25] tells us Moses assembled all the congregation of the children of Israel together. "They are the 600,000."[26] Without an infinite supply of souls, logic thus would seem to say that there could never be more than 600,000 souls within the Jewish nation, yet there certainly are more than 600,000 Jews in the world today.

Adam, whose very name means "man", was the repository of all the souls which ever would exist on earth.[27] His own soul thus was infinitely subdividable. When he sinned in Eden, the repository of the vessel was shattered and this corporate soul was fragmented into what the Kabbalist calls "sparks" — each one as unique as the microscopic double helix of DNA that determines every characteristic of the individual who receives it. Thus was the young earth sown with souls while millions more lay in metaphysical silos waiting their turn to begin the cycles of birth, life, death and birth again.

This explains why, though the Bible is explicit in numbering the Jews who followed Moses out of Egypt, the Jewish nation has found no shortage of souls for its growth through the centuries.

The concept of sparks also explains the varying psychological differences in mankind. With progress in modern science, we have become aware that the human organism is not just a physical structure made up of cells and molecules. We see today that at the elemental level we are made up of energy. And at the most internal level, an activity of intelligence is constantly going on in our bodies. If energy is the force behind our magnetic fields, then intelligence is the direction-giving influence of the force.

Every part of the body, even though it may appear solid and motionless, has continual activity taking place within it. Therefore, this infinite quantum of activity also contains an endless quantity of intelligence.

When the soul of Adam became fragmented, the endless amount of intelligences became incarnated in a body with its particular, microscopic DNA formula. Intelligences that were once part of Adam's brain incarnated as intelligent people whose work related to mind activity. Those intelligent forces that were part of Adam's fingers were corporealized as humans whose activities related to work with the fingers. Thus each and every single intelligence energy force of Adam's profile transmigrated with its peculiar and particular DNA formula accounting for the different people who inhabited the earth.

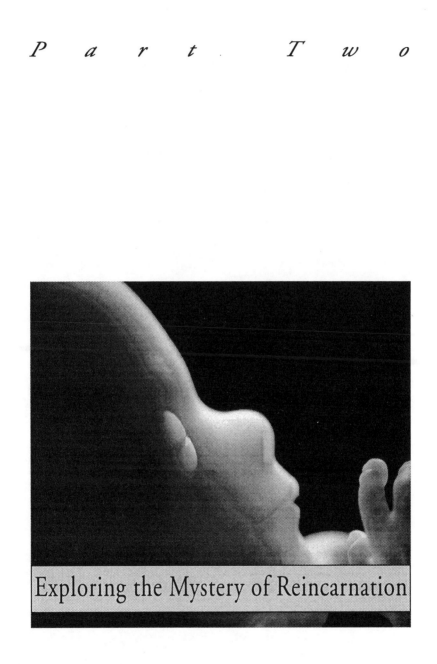

Exploring the Mystery of Reincarnation

8

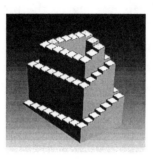

THE BODY AND INTERNAL FUNCTION

ANY DISCUSSION OF REINCARNATION MUST INCLUDE discussion of the origin of consciousness which implies pre-existence. But the concept can be clear only if we get away from the erroneous idea that consciousness must depend upon the physical brain. If that were the case, then consciousness, of necessity, would die when the body dies. Every individual, however, is comprised of two parts — the body function and the spiritual, or internal, function. The body may lapse into coma but the internal function may remain totally aware of what is happening — a point given great support by such "life after death" researchers as Elizabeth Kubler Ross whose subjects almost always report experiencing a long tunnel with a light at the end of it following clinical death and recovery.

Dr. Ross, however, was not the first to report the tunnel aspect. We are told in the Zohar that upon death of the physical body, the soul immediately travels to Hebron where Adam is and that it does so by means of a long tunnel.[28] This almost universally common experience, reported by Jews, Christians, agnostics and a broad cross section of other persuasions at the moment of clinical death, thus can scarcely be the product of a particular culture or religious bias. Logic would forbid that it be found in the DNA, and emphatically support the Kabbalist's contention that consciousness is immortal and will, in the course of time, return with all its memories intact, if inaccessible. Yet how many can remember details of their first year on earth? Fewer still can recall being one day old, yet every particular is there like the "BITS" in a computer's memory circuit. Any physicist will tell you that matter is energy and that energy cannot be destroyed. Thus, whatever happened in our lives — in this life or the last or the one preceding the last — remains stored and viable in the universe.

9

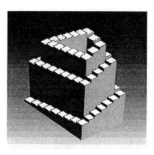

POWER OF THE MIND

CONSIDER A MIRACLE: TWO PEOPLE, BY MEANS OF SEXUAL intercourse, create another human being who comes into existence with all of his or her faculties and potentials in a total package on the day of birth. Without disputing the presence of God, why is the exercise of His power dependent upon the sexual passion of man. And if a child's moral, spiritual and mental abilities are present at birth. why are they so different in each individual? They range from the amorality and ignorance of the savage to the wisdom and ethic of the saint, and the differences in their destinies invariably are enormous. Obviously, pre-existence of the soul and an understanding of reincarnation alone can explain the differences which are measured by differences in behavior in past lives. The entire physical process of reproduction and birth is designed to supply the soul with a physical body that will conform to the behavior of that soul as it existed in a prior lifetime.

Reincarnation also sheds light on the subject of children who are born deformed, or who die when they still are very young, and those questions have tormented parents by the millions in every generation.

What is the purpose of such children? Why are so many of them born in city slums where the quality of life is minimal and hope almost nonexistent?

For the answer to that question in the case of every birth that has ever taken place or that ever will occur, look to one specific condition at one specific moment in time — the thoughts of the parents during sexual intercourse.

With body energy provided by the mother, whose metaphysical structure is negative, and soul energy channeled through the positive aspect of the father, the power of thought at the moment sperm is released will determine the lightness or heaviness of the child's body and spirit;[29] But thought will do even more. It will select the very soul that will occupy the body of their offspring by setting up the environmental conditions necessary for any given soul to meet its *tikune*.

A soul with a dark and heavy *tikune*, subject in reincarnation to live under the grim circumstances that might afford a chance of karmic balance, will home in swiftly upon conceptive thoughts of anger, frustration and destruction. The child born of that emotional union will display every one of its aspects.[30]

If the thoughts of a man and woman are of pure lust, motivated solely by the desire for self-indulgence, their child will reflect selfishness and lust, just as the child conceived in a moment of deep love and mutual understanding will reflect those positive characteristics. Because every soul, returning after death, must find a place in which conditions will be similar to those just left behind, parents virtually order their offspring as if picking them from a cosmic catalogue.

Thus, conception, ranging from the rage of forcible rape to the tenderness of righteous love-making will produce children ranging from the enraged to the righteous.

There are, of course, exceptions to the rule. Some few souls, *tikune* completed, return to this plane with a mission for mankind that has nothing to do with personal karma. Rabbi Shimon bar Yohai had no karmic reason to walk this earth 2000 years ago, but he alone could have revealed the wisdom of the Zohar.[31] Likewise, Rabbi Isaac Luria appeared solely to interpret the Zohar and spread its wisdom.[32]

10

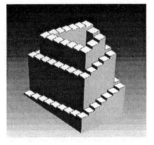

SOULMATES

FOR THE AVERAGE MAN OR WOMAN, HOWEVER, TO become parents is to open a channel for a soul that will enhance their lives or make them miserable depending upon their attitudes at the moment of that channel's creation. It is a frightening prospect and those who know nothing of Kabbalah or who dismiss reincarnation gamble with their very lives in the act of procreation.

Happy are those who may be soulmates in such a situation, for soulmates are truly one and are so happy in each other's company that no thought less than the most benign could intrude upon the act of making love.

In the Endless World, before Bread of Shame rose to cause restriction,[33] create darkness and result in the world in which we live, all souls were one. But the Zohar tells us that the Creator split each of them, creating male and female above before Adam and Eve were made manifest below.[34] Soulmates are those two halves of a single soul, back together again usually after wandering through many lifetimes searching for each other and fulfilling *tikune*.

As a general rule, soulmates may meet and marry only after the karmic debt has been paid, thus few in the world at any given time are soulmated. Still, men and women meet and marry, and not just for the sake of procreation.

Of the two sexes, men have the hardest time when it comes to making *tikune*. They are, perhaps, more willful and more stubborn than women who generally accomplish soul correction with as little as a single lifetime on this earth. When women return, karmic debt balanced, it is usually to aid a man who is struggling to balance his.[35] The aid is not always gentle. A man who has repeatedly failed to achieve soul correction may be given a woman who will make his life anything but pleasant. This would imply that when divorce and remarriage — often several times — occur, none of those unions are wasted. Every one of them was meant to be for the sake of whatever virtue a man must learn if it be one he will learn only through marriage.[36]

11

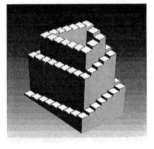

Reincarnation and Evil

WE LIVE A SERIES OF LIVES ON THIS EARTH, AND EACH incarnation is but a continuation of the preceding one. Thus, even a short life serves a purpose — be that purpose a lesson the soul of the child needs to learn or a lesson needed by the soul of the grieving parent. However tragic the circumstances may be, nothing is ever lost and nothing is ever forgotten. No matter how short or how tragic a life may be, it either adds something of value to the memory of the soul or it permits payment of a debt.

The meaning of reincarnation illuminates the problem of evil. Jew and Christian alike are taught that God is good, loving, just and all powerful. Yet who of us has not wondered why His world is filled with such misery and injustice? Religious leaders and philosophers alike have thrown up their hands at this seemingly unsolvable dilemma, but few, if any of them, have sought the answer in reincarnation.

The answer, of course, is that the degree of evil and

injustice abounding on this earth has nothing whatsoever to do with God. War, murder, violence, deceit and oppression are not the result of His will. Rather, they are the result of millions of souls struggling to balance their karmic debt and failing. Now, in the age of Aquarius, with time winding down to the coming of the Messiah and a passing away of the old order, souls laden with evil and in desperate need of correction before it is too late are flocking to this earth plane. Thus it is scarcely surprising that evil moves in high profile and that things seem worse than ever before.

Science, of course, unable to find empirical proof of reincarnation, rejects the obvious answer and continues to insist that crime is born solely of social and economic conditions and that human characteristics are exclusively the result of heredity. Yet while a child may look exactly like his or her parents, great differences in moral fiber and inherent attitude are frequently in evidence. These points cannot be explained in terms of heredity, nor can the fact that parents may seem to exercise great influence over one child and none whatsoever over another. The differences in human beings are not due to divine favoritism or the blind workings of the laws of physical heredity. Rather, they are based upon the differences between one soul and another. Such differences are never indiscriminately bestowed upon us. We, ourselves, bring our own characteristics into being. We are self-evolved. Evil is present so we can have choice between good and evil. Via free will we can get merit for our deeds. Otherwise, if only good existed, we would be automatons.

12

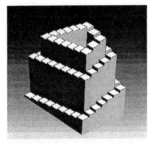

THE MAN WHO RETURNED AS HIS NEPHEW

NO OTHER SCIENCE STANDS TO BENEFIT MORE FROM the secrets of human reincarnation than do the various behavioral sciences which, for all of their advances in recent decades still stand baffled by the fact that thousands of hospital beds remain occupied by the so-called "mentally ill". Yet, for the time being at least, reincarnation still is frowned upon as unworthy of scientific inquiry, and it remains the perceived enemy of religion which fears its very essence as a threat to the prod of guilt. Yet there are case histories that illustrate its truth beyond mere argumentation of theory.

One such case began on a beautiful summer day in July 1979 when I received a frantic telephone call at our apartment in Ramat Gan in Israel.

"Our family must have an immediate appointment with you", cried Mrs. R.B., a student at our Beer Sheba centre. "The accidental death or the possible murder of our son and brother never ceases to haunt us and his mother has become increasingly morbid in her attitude towards life. She wants to know, once and for all, whether her son committed suicide, was intentionally murdered by his best friend, or was accidently shot by him".

The son, it developed, had been found dead eleven months before and after exhaustive investigation, the police had closed the file without coming to any conclusion as to the circumstances of his death.

I arranged a meeting at which all members of the immediate family would be present. I felt they would be necessary to provide any bits of information which, in most cases, appear to be of little or no significance, yet which often produce the missing parts of the human jigsaw puzzle. At the outset I made the point that our investigation would ultimately lead to a direct confrontation with the past 300 years of speculation regarding man's nature.

The ancient Kabbalistic position is that human beings consist of the mystical compound of physical matter and intangible spirit. For all the traditional resistance of their peers, prominent scientists[*] from fields as diverse as neurobiology and quantum physics recently have come out of the closet and admitted the possibility of such unscientific entities as the immortal human soul and a spiritually structured universe. Drawing from the Zohar[37] and Rabbi Isaac Luria's Gates of Reincarnation[38] I have come to the conclusion that the individuality of humans is not the result of their unique genetic code, but that the personal DNA structure is the result of the metaphysical, individual immortal soul that becomes manifest through the physical individual.

---

[*]Francis Crick, 1962 Nobel Prize-winner for physiology and medicine; Sir John Eccles, 1963 Nobel Prize-winner for physiology and medicine.

The same relationship exists between the seed and the tree. The entire potential state of the tree clearly exists in the seed long before it becomes manifest in leaves and branches.

Operating from that proposition, we started putting all the pieces together in an attempt to answer the question of the young man's tragic and untimely death.

Obviously most of the information that I was to gather in the course of our fact-finding mission would appear to have little significance or appear to be even remotely connected with the mystery. I was determined, however, that the immortal, nonmaterial intelligence of the soul was capable of influencing matter and that this would provide vital technical information as set down by the laws and principles of the *tikune* concept of reincarnation.

On Aug. 19, 1978 Aryeh, a soldier in the Israeli army and a resident of Beer Sheba, left his home with his closest friend to enjoy a day off and find some relief from the scorching summer heat. By 3:30 p.m., Aryeh was dead.

His friend was found on the road in a state of shock and confusion. He could tell a passerby only that his friend, Aryeh, lay dead of a gunshot wound, but how and why it happened would remain forever a mystery because he had no memory whatsoever of events leading up to the tragedy. A six-month police investigation shed no further light on the matter. Had Aryeh taken his own life? Was he accidently shot by his friend? Was he murdered? The police could not say. To learn the truth, the first thing I did was to ascertain the victim's correct Biblical name and his date of birth, based on the Hebrew lunar calendar.

I learned that Aryeh had been born on the ninth day of

the Hebrew month of *Heshvan* which, in that year, corresponded to the civil date of Nov. 12, 1958. The name Aryeh. in Hebrew, means lion and ironically he met his death in the cosmic month of Leo.

With no more than that upon which to base my investigation, I continued to ask members of his family one insignificant question after another in the hope that out of the maze would emerge the particular thought or event upon which our mystery might turn. It came when the brother of the deceased mentioned his son, saying he had named him after the slain Aryeh.

"What is the date of the birth of your son?" I asked.

"The 29th day in the Hebrew month of *Nissan*", he said.

I could scarcely restrain myself, because that was the clue for which I had been probing.

At that moment, I recalled a principle of the *tikune* process of reincarnation mentioned in the writings of the Ari in which he discusses the consequences of accidental murder[39] in light of the soul's knowledge of past lifetimes and their *tikune* requirements. Just as the physical DNA determines the color of an individual's eyes. the metaphysical DNA can determine commission of a murder.

"Why and what predetermines, directs and has brought into existence the circumstances surrounding the non-premeditated murder or accidental homicide?" asks the Ari. Based on a verse in Exodus, he concludes that accidental death may have already been predetermined and the circumstances that surround it are already known. The Bible states: "(If a man slay another) and the slayer lie not in wait but God cause it to come to hand, then I will appoint thee a place whither he may flee".[40]

The Ari notes that the passage contains an apparent contradiction. If the fatal blow was an accident, then what is meant by, "but God cause it to come to hand?". The passage implies that the slaying in question was predetermined by a prior intelligence.

Grappling with the metaphysical genetic code as a scientist grapples with the forces directing the growth and behavior of physical living systems, the Ari daringly states that the victim cited was already a condemned man before the slaying and that the accident was an opportunity to provide the victim with the earliest possible reincarnation.

"Furthermore", says the Ari, "through the methodology of Kabbalistic letters, the appropriate time for non-premeditated murder victims to return for *tikune* purposes is during the Hebrew month of *Elul* (Virgo)".[41] In his revolutionary study of the *tikune* process, the Ari established a framework of the metaphysical DNA code that was profoundly influential upon the environmental as well as upon the biological processes.

Since Aryeh had not reached his 20th birthday, this was indicative of the fact that he could not have met his death as a result of wrongdoing on his part since, according to Talmudic interpretation[42] anyone below the age of 20 cannot be condemned to death for premeditated murder. His death, therefore, could only have been the result of a principle in the *tikune* process of reincarnation.

I therefore proceeded to calculate the time of conception of the child born to Aryeh's brother following his death, and to my surprise I found that conception had to have occurred in the month of *Elul.* The child, Aryeh, was born on the civil date of April 26, 1979 or the Hebrew date of the 29th of *Nissan,* making the date of conception in the month of *Elul.* That, plus the fact that the child was named Aryeh, indicated that the two Aryehs were the same, with the elder reincarnated in the form of his own brother's son.

That conclusion, and the circumstances surrounding it, answered the grieving family's question. Their son did not commit suicide, nor was he the victim of a premeditated slaying. The proof of that point lay in the conception of a new, yet old, Aryeh in the Hebrew month of *Elul,* along with the naming of the child after the victim — a direct result formulated by the *tikune* process through which the superior metaphysical intelligence of the soul structures the environmental as well as the biological process of evolvement and development.

The effect of this explanation upon the family was profound. The spirit of the deceased and newly born Aryeh produced a moral awareness of sufficient intensity as to alter their lives and make them more loving toward each other.

A final point of proof that no suicide was involved could be applied only to the concept of reincarnation. The Zohar[43] states that suicide is a crime punishable by death. In a physical sense the old Aryeh had died but was now alive in the spirit of the young child who bore his name.

13

RECALLING PAST LIVES

PERHAPS NOW WE CAN SEE THAT REINCARNATION IS intrinsic to each of us and that it is incumbent upon all of us to use its precepts to enhance the fruits of our lives. There are many avenues by which enhancement can be achieved, and memory is one of them. In fact, recall of past lives is the one overwhelming proof of the validity of reincarnation. It also is the most difficult proof to achieve, since few of us can summon such recall at will. Yet, the fact that we cannot remember a prior existence is no more proof that a past life did not exist than not being able to remember what we had for breakfast last week is proof that we did not eat it. Most of us cannot recall the first four years of our lives, even though those four years are the most important years of all in formation and development of what we are to be in the years that remain.

According to the Zohar,[44] the mind, or the physical brain if you will, never forgets anything. There is no disappearance in any matter concerning metaphysics or the spirit. Just as satellites today monitor and record almost everything that moves on earth, so is the brain an all-seeing camera that records everything that takes place in its owner's lifetime.

The problem lies, as the computer technicians would say, in "accessing the data". Efforts to achieve that access have taken two dominant forms in recent decades. One of them works, the other does not. That which does is not hypnotism.

Hypnosis gained great respectability as a tool with which to probe past lives a number of years ago when a young researcher "regressing" a patient back through her life allegedly pushed her beyond birth and discovered "Bridie Murphy". Under hypnosis, the woman with whom he was dealing gave a detailed account of a prior lifetime in Ireland, recalling facts she could not have known and even speaking in Gaelic, a language she never had studied.

The world was electrified at news of the event, but subsequent investigation eventually discounted the entire scenario. We do not have space here to repeat details of what came to be known as "The Search for Bridie Murphy", but even without it, logic would dictate that hypnosis, in its formal sense, never could produce a true out of body experience. Once an individual is out of the body and no longer governed by the precepts of time, space and motion he has access to time not governed by this plane of existence. The individual under hypnosis may feel disassociation with the body, but he is still responding to questions and suggestions of the inquirer. The connection of physical words can never come through the astral body. Only if there is a complete subjugation of the physical body — a complete negation of it — can knowledge of past incarnations be realized.

One method that does work is meditation, whether it is

used to explore past lives, to pray effectively or merely to relax and escape the perils of tension by relaxing the body, quieting the mind and turning off the incessant flow of inward chatter with which the mind is constantly inundated.

There are enough forms and variations of Kabbalistic meditation to fill a book of its own, but without going into specifics, a general profile of the practice can be offered here.

A good way to begin any meditation is to spend a few minutes silently asking, "What do I want?" Since on a surface level most of us would be quick to say we know what we want it is a question seldom asked and rarely answered, but eventually it will lead one to control one's mind and open the door to a higher cosmic consciousness.

Most of us go through life allowing our bodies, like the robots they are, to handle virtually every function of living, but there is a soul within and with very little effort it can seize control. It is much like a man out walking his dog. The dog, if not brought to heel, walks ahead and appears to be leading, but he constantly stops and looks back to be sure his master is following. The same thing applies to the body and the soul, and with just a little determination, the soul can leave the body to journey back in time.

The Zohar has long maintained what Elizabeth Kubler Ross and her colleagues recently have affirmed in their studies of clinical death and recovery — that when the soul leaves the body it travels through a long tunnel.

According to the Zohar,[45] that tunnel leads to Hebron in Israel and the cave of Machpelah where Abraham, Isaac, Jacob and even Adam and Eve lie buried. But one does not have to be physically dead to traverse it. Any out-of-body experience gained through meditation takes the soul over the same route.

Therefore, to make the move back into time and into other incarnations, the meditator needs only to envision the tunnel, being sure only that he stops as soon as he sees light at its nether end. To go all the way and leave the tunnel where the light marks its boundary is to leave the body in death, consequently, there is a potential measure of danger in this meditation. Some reportedly have been unable to return, but I personally have known only one person who experienced difficulty in getting back and the method, if prudently handled is one of the best.

Even without meditation, however, our lives abound with clues as to what has gone before and one of the most telling of those clues is the experience of fear.

Almost all of us are plagued by one or more irrational, unfounded fears. Heights give us vertigo, tight places afflict us with claustrophobic panic, the sight of a cat sets us to trembling. Such phobias in some unfortunate individuals become so intense as to coalesce into one great pantophobia so crippling that its victims cannot bear even to leave their homes.

"Unfounded" is an excellent adjective because it means we have not yet "found" the reason for such fears, but they are an excellent indication of events in a prior incarnation. While any victim understandably would like to be free of phobias, they should not be driven out by therapy until they have been closely examined for they contain valuable information.

Even as any meditation should begin with the question, "What do I want?" a meditation to overcome phobia should begin with the question, "Why do I really have this fear?".

Simply asking the question plants the seed of the answer. But what is hidden is not the information itself. What is hidden is the desire to request the information. Dig it out and you will begin to make progress toward alleviation of the fear through the memory of what caused it. To relive is to relieve.

14

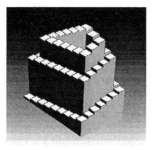

BREAKING THE CODE

THE ZOHAR SAYS[46] "IT IS NOW FITTING TO REVEAL
mysteries connected with that which is above and that which is
below". Thus do we learn that the Torah is a code. It conceals.
The Zohar says[47] "Now there is no work of the Holy One so
recondite but he has recorded it in the Torah. And the Torah has
revealed it in an instant. Then straightaway clothes it with another garment so that it is hidden there and does not show itself.
But the wise whose wisdom makes them full of eyes peers
through the garment to the very essence of the word that is hidden nearby. And when the word is momentarily revealed in that
first instant of which we have spoken, those whose eyes are wise
can see it, though it is so soon hidden again".

Hebrew is not merely a language for Jewish conversation.
Every word is a vessel of power and energy. Even translated into
English, much of the meaning remains. We read in the Zohar:[48]
"And the letter *Beth* came before the Creator and said, 'My Lord,
I find it best for you to create within me this entire world because

within me the entire world will be blessed, both the upper and the lower world, for the letter Beth signifies blessing'. And the Holy One answered and said, 'For surely through you I shall create the world and you shall be the beginning of creation and within you shall be the entire creation".

It is difficult to understand how a letter — a Hebrew letter — can be a vehicle for the creation of an entire world, but one needs only to take a look at a seed to determine whether it is the seed of a man or an apple tree. What we observe in this minute element is that by planting either seed, the effects will be enormous in its infinite potential. If we were to take a relatively simple word such as that of a computer, and describe everything it represents to us we would be able to fill volumes with our descriptions.

Of all the multifaceted experiences through which we have gone and of all the thoughts that have thronged the corridors of our minds, what remains? Usually a fleeting recollection — a summary — at best, and only by such recollections and summaries are we aware that we have gone through any sort of experience at all. Yet through those experiences, lessons drawn are indelibly etched upon the consciousness whether the etching tool is remembered or not.

Have you ever wondered, when you are reading, how it is that you can grasp the ideas conveyed by the printed words? At what point did you actually learn about word meaning and sentence structure: The specific is unimportant and the mind probably has thrown it out with the trash. The important fact is that you can read.

The average person is well aware that if he puts his finger into an electrical socket, he will get a shock, but the chances are good that he long since has forgotten whatever experience it was — vivid as it must have been at that moment — that taught him the lesson. He needs no recall of the experience so long as the underlying lesson remains. The point holds true with regard to virtually every facet of the personality. Just as we have learned not to jeopardize fingers with electrical sockets, we have learned not to lie or cheat or steal. We may have had to learn and relearn some of these lessons in order to make them part of us, but if the lessons remain, the means by which the lesson was acquired is immaterial.

The same point holds for reincarnation. To argue that because there is no recall of past lives, past lives never existed is like contending that radio waves do not exist because they cannot be seen. Recall of past incarnations may not lie at our fingertips, but they are there. All we have to do to reach them is to clean out the rust that has accumulated within our metaphysical computers. With memory restored, we can recall and understand past incarnations and thus clarify and explain the present one.

We have lost the ability to see things as they really are, and with that loss has gone the ability to become fully acquainted with our past lives. As a result, we plunge blindly through the present one using information gained in the past without the slightest awareness that we are applying it.

If heredity were the only key to human behavior, identical twins would behave in identical fashion, yet in any given set of twins, one may turn to art and the other to mathematics. One may be lazy while the other cannot be constrained. It is the differences that lead one to questions about the impact of heredity and the input of reincarnation. Of the two, it is reincarnation that provides most of the answers parents have sought when, in one way or another, their children have gone astray. This information can relieve a world of useless guilt.

The paradox of divergence between parent and child is an ancient one.

In the Bible[49] we are told: "Now these are the generations of Terah — Terah begat Abram, Nachor and Charan..." Terah, then, was the father of Abraham, yet the sages of the Talmud say that Terah was an idol worshipper and a wicked man. How, then, could he sire a son who would grow up to be the father of the Jewish nation? Abraham was so pure and wonderful, so intelligent and enlightened that he learned to combine the physical world with the metaphysical world and operate in each — a feat accomplished by only six of those who followed him: Isaac, Jacob, Joseph, Moses, Aaron and David. How could a man so mean of mind and spirit as Terah thus found such a dynasty?

The Torah[50] gives us a reverse of the situation in Jacob and Esau even as they grew in Rebekah's womb: "And the children struggled together within her and she said, 'If it be so, why am I thus?'. And she went to inquire of the Lord. And the Lord said unto her, 'Two nations are in thy womb, and two manners of people shall be separated from thy bowels and the one people shall be stronger than the other people and the elder shall serve the younger'...And when her days to be delivered were fulfilled, behold there were twins in her womb". This tale of Rebekah is a cloak concealing the innermost secrets of our universe and of man or, to put it another way, the secrets of reincarnation and of the guiding forces behind every human event. It provides clarification of that all-too-common situation with a family in which two brothers hate each other, or a son hates his father, or a mother and daughter are at odds. The probability is that they really are in no way related. Instead, the principals are merely acting out a vendetta begun and nurtured in a past life to be carried over for conclusion in this one.

P a r t   T h r e e

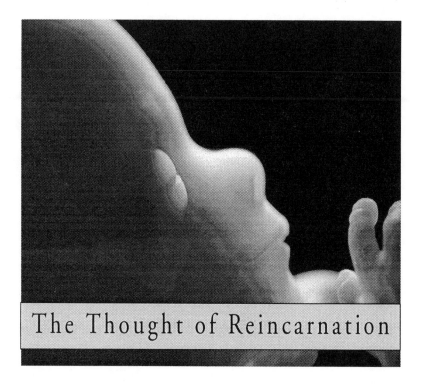

The Thought of Reincarnation

15

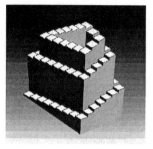

THE PURPOSE OF REINCARNATION

THERE ARE MANY SCHOOLS OF THOUGHT AS TO THE purpose of reincarnation. That it is for improvement of the soul is obvious, but some would add that education of the soul and the soul's inherent desire for growth are equally important. But such is not the case. Experience is the driving force that brings us back. It is the seed of the desire for knowledge, the yearning to mingle in the rush of physical existence which is based upon the desire for education.

To many whose lives are dreary and difficult, the soul's desire for growth might seem inconceivable, but it is only satiety that brings about a lack of desire. Thus, an end to the cycle of reincarnation can be expected only when the soul has grown sufficiently that it no longer has desire for rebirth. Our waking consciousness is only a portion of our actual consciousness. Our deeper selves often realize the need of that about which our superficial selves care little.

Those who do not know of Kabbalah may reason that physical consciousness, being limited in outlook to the narrow horizon of a single earthlife, does not desire to be reborn, but soul consciousness, having a splendid goal in view, is anxious to return.

From a Kabbalistic viewpoint, just the opposite is true. It is the soul's desire to remain in its pure state of consciousness, without having to resort to physical existence in a body with all its limitations, that resists rebirth.

The soul is a metaphysical force which creates life within us. When the soul leaves the body, it creates death because there is no life in the body itself. Thus soul and body are in a constant state of struggle.

When we speak of the body and of the soul, however, we are not speaking of physical energies. The body is a physical entity, but there is a motivating force within it — something beyond the operation of cells and genetic makeup that makes it grow and function. The force is called body energy which can be defined only as the "Desire to Receive for Itself Alone",[51] which is the root of all evil.

This body energy can be deactivated only if it can be integrated with something that is similar to itself and thus become part of the whole and lose its separate identity. Its energy is the same as the energy of the earth which, with the grip of its gravity, desires to swallow everything in its reach. Thus does the body forever attempt to revert back to its true home, which is the earth.

Only the soul provides the force which can integrate body energy into the whole and convert the whole to a "Desire to

Receive for the Sake of Imparting",[52] and when that occurs, the soul has fulfilled its destiny by balancing its *tikune*. When that happens, the body dies. But in a truly righteous person body energy and soul energy become indistinguishable and disintegration of the body is no longer necessary. For most, the body must disintegrate because as long as it exists it can maintain its hold on the soul which, perhaps, has earned its release. A righteous person's body is no longer wrapped in evil and, in fact, does not decay, even in the grave.

As a metaphysical entity, however, the soul — whether it has achieved correction or not — has no inherent desire to dwell in the body's linear, mundane world and, once there, inevitably wishes to depart. Psychiatrists have a label for this phenomenon, shared to greater or lesser degree by all of us.

They call it "the death wish". The description is accurate. They simply do not know its origin which best can be described as conflict between two opposing views of the world.

The soul's view of the world is anchored in a Desire to Receive for the Sake of Sharing, and this view is translated as the goodness found in one quantity or another in almost all who breathe. The body, however, exists solely to receive for itself alone. It eats. It drinks. It hoards. It indulges its solitary vices and shares with no one. Even the inexorable gravitational pull of the earth upon which it walks feeds its desire, pulling the soul down, restricting and constraining it. Nervous or mental breakdowns, in the Kabbalistic view, are but manifestations of this constant battle between the body's Desire to Receive and the soul's yearning to impart. When the body overwhelms the soul, it shuts off the flow of positive energy without which the soul cannot survive. Usually the last words of a suicide are, "I can't take it". When the soul can no longer "take" what life has to give on its own terms, it must depart.

Indeed, it is probable that none of us would survive had sleep not been given to us. And what a gift it is! Only during those hours of physical inactivity can the soul leave the body, returning each night to the place of its origin to be recharged for the combat to follow when sleep is done. Without sleep, the body would destroy the soul in short order.

The point needs no metaphysical argument as proof. It has been empirically proven, in experiment and in human experience. People deliberately submitting themselves to sleep deprivation often begin to hallucinate. Emotions become frenzied. Physical coordination vanishes. Similarly, those who suffer from insomnia find themselves exhausted even though they have remained in bed eight hours every night.

The problem is less a question of sleep deprivation than of dream deprivation, for dreams are manifestations of cosmic consciousness in which all knowledge flows, free of the body's greed. Only in the cosmic realm entered during sleep can the soul receive the periodic recharging it needs in order to remain functional. In the process, the soul frequently relives past incarnations, often converting their events into revelatory dream symbols as the soul roams freely outside the constraints of time, space and motion.

The soul, upon entering the body, is like a man put in prison. It is confined — unable to exert its influence as it might desire. It is bound to conform to the laws and principles of the physical universe even as a prisoner is bound to the law of the prison. But only here can it ever hope to complete its *tikune* and thereby earn eternal rest and purification in the cosmic world in the presence of its Creator.

Therefore, it can be seen that desire for education or soul

growth are not the motivating factors that draw a soul to this world again and again.

16

FREE WILL

THERE ARE MANY REASONS FOR REINCARNATION, BUT one of the soul's central motives is its hunger for free will. Its origin is as old as time itself. One of the fundamental principles of Kabbalah is a condition known as "Bread of Shame".[53] We all ate of it in the Endless World, when our souls were created long before there were any stars or planets or galaxies.

Our souls were created for one reason only — the Creator, in whom all things are invested, had a Desire to Share. But when the Creator existed alone, sharing could not occur. There were no vessels to hold the endless bounty pouring out of Him and so, with nothing more than desire, He created those vessels, which are our souls to this day, as the living Desire to Receive from His exalted light.

For time beyond our linear comprehension, our souls did just that. They received with no motive other than to receive for themselves alone. But as they were filled, a new yearning evolved

— one that put them on a collision course with the Creator. Suddenly, in emulation of the Creator, our souls developed a Desire to Receive for the Purpose of Sharing. But they were faced with the same dilemma as that which faced the Creator Himself before He created his vessels. With every soul filled, there was no one and nothing with whom to share.

Thus — "Bread of Shame". Shame at receiving so much and giving nothing in return. Shame at being in a position in which the soul had no opportunity to say yes or no to the Creator and, by that exercise of will, prove itself worthy to receive and thus dispel the shame.

The shame led to rebellion — a mass rejection of the Creator's beneficence. When that happened, the light was withdrawn, darkness and the unclean worlds were created and all became finite — or limited — and thus in need of receiving.[54] With those worlds came these clay bodies — vessels desiring only to receive for themselves alone — in which our souls reside. Here they forever struggle against body energy, to share.

Thus it can be seen that the soul desires a body and a sojourn in this limited world, not for the experience or the education, but for the sole purpose of being in a position of choice — to be able to say to the Creator, "I have a Desire to Receive either for Myself Alone or for the Purpose of Sharing, and I can exercise either option as I choose." When we choose to selfishly exercise the body's desire, we cut off all beneficence from the Creator, but at least the choice is free.

In the Endless World, the soul had no choice to make, and no opportunity to share since all souls there were full. In this limited world, however, there are many others with whom to share or reject as we so desire. By entering this world, the soul has the opportunity to struggle against body energy that says, "don't share with anyone, receive for yourself alone", and in so doing, prove its worth.

Learning to share, with rejection of greed that says, "take it all", thus became the soul's mission in life — and in life after life after life, depending upon the soul's progress toward that goal. Kabbalistically speaking, attaining that goal is called making a *tikune* or correction of the soul.

There is nothing automatic in the aspect of sharing. It can only be done as a function of free and conscious will. A man who is drinking a cup of coffee from a cup with a hole in the bottom from which much of the coffee is flowing is not sharing that which he does not drink. To give up part of the coffee — to share it — he must have control over all of it and an opportunity to say either, "I'll save some for somebody else", or "No, I'll keep it all for myself". Having no control over it, he neither accepts nor rejects (shares) it.

This concept lies at the heart of Judaism. But in the Kabbalistic view it has nothing to do with religion. It is not so much a case of putting faith in God as in putting faith in a system that teaches us how to receive. "Receive" is the literal meaning of "Kabbalah",[55] but faith has little to do with reincarnation.

We, not fate, dictate every event of our lives. Heavy negative influences — and all of us encounter them at one time or another — are not a cause for despair, but only a warning that one must walk cautiously and avoid unnecessary risk in a dangerous period. But from a Kabbalistic — even from a karmic — viewpoint, the individual is always in control. When pain, suffering and tragedy attend us, it is only because we have mandated them in a previous incarnation and must now remove the defects they represent so that our souls can progress.

There is no such thing as punishment in the *tikune* process. Its sole purpose is to move a soul toward purification.

The world is full of those who have borne its attendant pain with nobility. Helen Keller, though deaf and blind, probably had more fulfillment in her life than most of us who have ears but cannot hear and eyes but cannot see.

This life is only one station. It is not the full road and 70 or 120 years on this earth is but the wink of an eye. The only reason for a soul's desire to sojourn on this earth is the opportunity to earn the right to receive beneficence from the Creator. Rarely is that right won in a single lifetime.

17

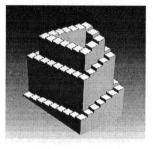

METAPHYSICAL CIRCUITRY

WHENEVER WE RECEIVE WITH THE INTENTION OF sharing, we are rejecting part of what is received, thus creating resistance. This in turn creates the vessel by which the energy of the soul is revealed. That energy is not created; it is there, all the time, waiting to fill the soul.

When the Creator's beneficence first was rejected in the Endless World, Light, which is to say energy, withdrew — not in the sense of movement, for in the metaphysical sense light is a constant that never moves — but through lack of a vessel to reveal it. If a room is dark, it means only that no one has thrown the switch to complete the electrical circuit and reveal the light. The light is there, waiting. The atoms are there and the whole structure of energy is there, but only when the switch is thrown is the vessel that will reveal it created.

Thus all souls have a single and common purpose when they enter a body for a brief walk through this or that lifetime.

They are in that earth plane to create vessels that will reveal the light. The energy is already within us, but if it goes unrevealed, we are unsatisfied. The minute we create a vessel that reveals the light, we are satisfied.

We can create the necessary circuit of energy only when a resistance factor is involved. The resistance factor — whether it is found in a simple electrical circuit or a soul — creates the returning light from the positive pole which, in turn, creates feasibility of acceptance. Creation of vessels is accomplished when we exercise our free will to observe the precepts as dictated in the Bible, and the metaphysical energy released as a result of our actions accomplishes the *tikune* for which we have been reincarnated.

Unspiritual as it may sound, we are here for no other purpose than to receive. We seek fulfillment now because, burdened by Bread of Shame, we refused fulfillment in the Endless World at the time of creation. The degree of our desire to receive it now is the only difference between one soul and another. The method by which one goes about achieving what one desires is the sole morality.

Unhappily, all established religions preach the effect without seeking the purpose. They place a great deal of emphasis on telling their followers what to do without telling them why they should do it. They tell their adherents to be "good", and if one asks why, they will say "because it is in the Bible". But why is it in the Bible, and what does the Bible have to say to each individual soul regarding its own peculiar and individualistic need? Established religions answer in generalities but overlook the only general rule that can apply to all. It is, simply, that each and every one of us is a communications system whose purpose it is to draw metaphysical energy from the Creator, thereby fulfilling His desire to share. Like any system known to science and technology, we must complete our energy circuit by means of a positive, negative and central column.[56] It is that system that was lost to us in the Endless World. The need to regain that system within our individual souls is what keeps us coming back to this earth plane again and again.

In the Endless World, the vessel and the light were equals in that the light created the action and the vessel created the equal opposite reaction. Yet there was one difference between them. The light created the vessel, but the vessel did not create a vessel. The light created a vessel to enhance itself but the vessel, which was merely the receiver of this action, could not create.

Bread of Shame was the result of our inability to create. The vessels — all the souls in creation — said to the Creator, "No — you can use us as vessels only if we, the vessels, can create the vessel that will reveal you and thus share with you even as you share with us".

Thus did God create man in His own image, because man, in the Endless World, demanded it. He said, "I want to be as close to you as possible. And I am close to you in all respects save this: I am the vessel you created to reveal yourself, but Bread of Shame forbids that I continue to reflect and reveal you until I can create the vessel whereby this is done".

This, perhaps, is the reason why, to this day, some men have more regard for a computer than for their own brains. In creating the computer, man has created a vessel to reveal himself, whereas his brain remains a vessel created by God.

But why, to return to a subject far more grim than the joyous desire to reveal and share, do such violent and heinous crimes as murder scar the landscapes of our existence and why do they tempt each of us, in fantasy if nothing else, from time to time. The reason is simple. Each of us must have the opportunity to say no.

Without conscience or morality, to kill a competitor in business, for example, might make perfectly good sense. After all, if one kills his competitor, he will be in a position to gain more energy, in the form of money or profit, will he not?

The flaw in that logic is not a point of conscience or morality, however. Kabbalistically speaking, there can be no such thing as murder for gain, simply because gain can never result from murder.

In the Endless World, we existed as vessels whose sole function was to reveal the Creator by receiving his beneficence. But that system worked only until the advent of Bread of Shame when we rejected that beneficence, refusing to receive unless we could share and thus create a vessel of our own.

Thus, whenever one kills, he is taking another's energy without first creating a vessel in which to hold it. The only way in which he can create such a vessel is to reject murder. Without a vessel, one can never hold what the act of murder might bring. The energy thus taken remains with the murderer until, in the current, or a future lifetime, an appropriate vessel is created to contain it and relieve him of his burden.

Even money inherited from birth falls under these precepts. Without charity — without the creation of a vessel by means of sharing a percentage — its internal energy cannot be held.

An inherited fortune, unlike money gained by means of

murder or other violent action, is legitimate, yet it still contains the Bread of Shame if all it does is to fulfill the Desire to Receive for the Self Alone. Bread of Shame whispers, "Look at all the potential energy of that money. It's not yours and having that money does not make you any better than the person who has no money".

In order to secure this energy given from birth, one must establish companionship, friendship and intimacy with one's fellow man. Only through such intimacy can a Desire to Receive for the Sake of Sharing be established. The inheritor cannot fulfill his soul with money. The soul does not eat money. It only eats internal energy and it can have that only by sharing the money.

Many a man labors all his life to purchase a home in which he seldom lives because he is so busy with his continuing labors. Why would a man work so hard for a home and then have so little real desire to occupy it? It is because the energy of the money he made to purchase that home never really went into it. What was transferred from the purchaser to the original owner was money, but not the energy of the money. Whether the money used in the purchase was earned or inherited, the energy it contains cannot be revealed without a new vessel. Simply receiving the vessel that was already there, will reveal nothing. There is no joining of the energy unless some of it is transferred to charity. When that transfer is made, a new vessel has been created, but that can be done only by including somebody else. It is for this reason that the Bible[57] commands man to give a tithe amounting to 10% of his yearly earnings. By freely volunteering the money to charity, he creates the vessel to contain and maintain the other 90% of his earnings.

18

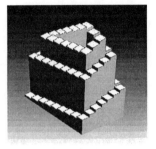

THE DIVINE EQUITY

THERE ARE CIRCUMSTANCES UNDER WHICH A SOUL will return to this earth plane solely for the purpose of helping someone else grow and fulfill the purpose of one's own incarnation. Sometimes the soul in question will accomplish that mission by creating misery so as to reinstate a situation that existed in a prior lifetime, thus giving the soul to be tested a choice as to how it will behave.

It is possible that a soul being unkind to another is doing so because the other soul had been unkind to him in a prior lifetime. Thus a murder victim never really is a "victim" in the sense of reincarnation. Invariably, he is one who committed murder in a prior lifetime and is paying for it here.

Another example of the use of a soul to punish other souls for the sake of their growth and correction may be seen in the death of a child. Returning to pay back debts incurred in a prior lifetime does not apply to a child under the age of 13, but if the child dies at that tender age, it is possible that he was here only to create necessary anguish for the people who are his parents so that through that anguish they might correct a defect incurred in this or a prior lifetime. It stands to reason that any soul which lives in the body past the age of 13 is here for its own *tikune*. Prior to that, it is here only to set a scene.

Good scenery is essential to a good play. If we are not able to see how the death of a child has affected the individual grief stricken because of it, it is only because of our own limited experience in viewing. Names and dates and external things may have changed, but internally that individual is behaving as he has always behaved in lifetimes past. As he is led to some climax in this life, it will seem new to him because so few of us are able to remember prior incarnations, but he will be propelled toward that climax by his body. Bodies are not souls, but they play a very important part in the show.

Above all else, understanding of the laws of *tikune* — also known as the laws of karma — can be achieved only through the practice of Kabbalistic meditation techniques. Karma, which operates on a mental and moral plane, is a principle of cause and effect. The law of karma decrees that for every action there must be an equal corresponding reaction so that ultimately we all will receive exactly what we have solicited. A universal grasp and understanding of the nature of the law of *tikune* could change the entire world.

If people could accept the truth of the proverb[58] which says, "Cast thy bread upon the waters for thou shalt find it after many days", the world would be a different place in which to live. It means simply that the practice of goodness and kindness will be rewarded unexpectedly after a long interval. It means that whatever one plants, that is what he will reap.

If people really accepted this principle, they would be far less inclined to exploit their fellows on this planet, and the idea of "love thy neighbor"[59] would be regarded as a practical rule of thumb rather than as a remote ideal. We then would know that the only thing we can take with us beyond the grave is that which we have given away.

A modern bank is an excellent example of this precept. The bank itself does not dispense money. The bank customer may withdraw only that which he, himself, has placed in the bank earlier. When a person takes a loan from the bank, it is understood that he must repay it. In effect, he has taken something that doesn't belong to him since he has taken something out of this life which he has not yet earned. In keeping with the laws of cause and effect and action and reaction, repayment must follow.

If we choose to cast our bread upon the waters because, like the bank customer, we intend to draw upon it at some future time, or if we have taken credit in this life with the expectation of ultimately paying for it, we must still operate under the law of tikune. It exists solely for the purpose of repayment.

A single incarnation, however, may not show the manner in which an individual receives what he has given. Nor does it necessarily provide payment for a credit which has been extended.

To clarify the point, let us remember that the purpose of our being here is to fill ourselves. When we speak of a short circuit, we speak of someone who has received energy without removing his Bread of Shame. We are, in effect, saying he has gone through a life without repayment for what he has received. He may have been paid for all the good he has done in this lifetime, but he has not paid for all the evil he has done. That is why we frequently see those who are enjoying success and good fortune they obviously have not earned. But this life is only one of many chapters. In a subsequent incarnation, they will pay for their evil in full.

Adolf Eichmann, finally seized and tried in Israel for his crime years after World War II, defended his heinous actions with the excuse, "I was only following orders". Lieutenant Calley said the same thing of the massacre he led at My Lai village in Vietnam. Kabbalistically speaking, we must lay aside our outrage at so lame a reason for massive bloodshed and ask why those two souls were placed in a position to decide whether or not they should follow such orders. The respective roles of these two men — one a German Nazi, the other an American officer — patently were roles of massive *tikune*. Most cases are not so obvious.

As we move into the age of Aquarius, there are very few souls that have not been incarnated at one time or another.[60] The law of *tikune*, therefore, is really the law of fair play. By permitting a soul to sojourn in the physical world, it is given an opportunity to correct misdeeds, performed in a previous lifetime.

In a prior lifetime, one may have been a bank robber who caused several deaths. In this lifetime, he might be a famous surgeon and use his skill to save several lives. If he can escape the built-in ego traps inherent in such a situation to use his skill for the benefit of others, realizing it is only a tool and not a manifestation of his own glory, he may be able to correct the evil wrought in a prior lifetime.

It is unfortunate that it usually takes far more lifetimes to complete a tikune than might be required if we would only grasp the problem and apply ourselves to it instead of dwelling in unhappiness over some imagined injustice. We usually avoid taking advantage of lessons taught in our daily lives unless we are forced by bitter experience to examine them. Usually, these lessons must be patiently repeated day after day, year after year — even lifetime after lifetime — until the knowledge we have ignored comes crashing in on us, sometimes in a most devastating fashion. But if we can learn to cooperate with the strings of the universe and its steadfast onward movement of evolution instead of stubbornly resisting it, our spiritual growth would blossom.

It also is unfortunate that so few of us wish to take advantage of the memory of experiences through which we have gone since in those experiences lies all wisdom, the reasons for our existence and our educational tools. But many of us are prohibited from delving into our own natures by fear of what we may find there.

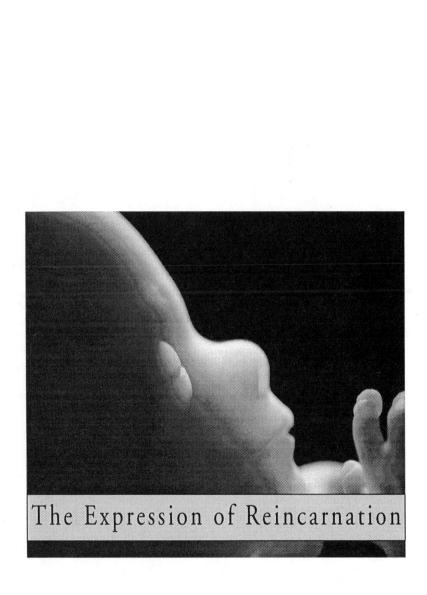

The Expression of Reincarnation

19

STRUCTURE OF THE SOUL

THE DESIRE TO RECEIVE FOR ONESELF ALONE IS A universal tendency. But this selfishness is a distortion and a warped reflection of the light we are here to receive. The Ari[60] makes it clear that before a person can know and abide by the laws of *tikune*, he must know the root and place of his soul.

To know that, however, one must first know the structure within which root and place are to be found. Like so much in the world of metaphysics, that structure is a triad. It consists of *Nefesh*, which is the realm of crude spirit; *Ruah*, which is the realm of spirit more refined; and *Neshamah*, which is the realm of the true soul.

The soul within the realm of *Nefesh* is more closely aligned with body energy and is materialistic in nature. One who dwells there never has enough of anything and displays little sensitivity to the needs and desires of others. He seeks nothing beyond the gratification of his own ego.

Through the process of *tikune*, a soul eventually may reach the level of *Ruah* in which it still has hungers and desires but is no longer ruled by them. With consideration for others, it will bypass certain things if they can be had only at the expense of his fellows. The soul at the level of *Ruah* is fertile ground for the first green growth of true charity.

At the top of the spiritual triad lies *Neshamah*. The inherent desire to receive still dwells there but it is totally subordinate to the individual's desire to share. There can be little mystery as to what level any soul has attained because the individual will quickly manifest its characteristics.

Some few souls at the fall of Adam escaped the corruption of the evil shells we call *klippot* and from time to time, they will appear to guide us along the perilous way of lives, but for most of us, existence is a struggle to climb out of self-centered *Nefesh*, through *Ruah* to *Neshamah*.

The Zohar[61] says, "Praiseworthy are those who indulge in the Torah to know the wisdom of their law, and furthermore they know and reflect upon the upper internal secrets when man leaves this world. For through a death, when he has done repentance... it removes the harsh judgment of this world"

Thus it is through reflection that a person knows the laws of his law and knows himself. By understanding the karmic law, one will know how he will have to give an account of his deeds to the supernal Creator. One must also know and reflect upon the secrets of the Zohar — Why has a soul come into this particular body? Why has this body received the grade of soul that occupies it? On what foundation does this world stand? How must one share in its correction?

Anyone who goes to the future world without knowing the mysteries of the Torah wherein the mysteries of the soul are revealed, will be barred from all the gates of the future world however great his deeds may be.[62]

The Song of Songs[63] says, "Tell me, O thou whom my soul loves, where thou makest thy flock to rest at noon". The Zohar says[64] this is the soul speaking to the Creator saying, "tell me the mysteries of the supernal wisdom; how do you lead your flock in the upper world? Teach me some of the mysteries of the wisdom for I have not learned them. Teach me so I will not be in shame when I come to be among the eternal souls, for until now I have not reflected on these mysteries". And the Song of Songs continues with the response of the Creator, "If thou knowest not, oh thou fairest of women, go thy way forth by the footsteps of the flock, and feed thy kids beside the shepherds' tents".

The Zohar[65] interpretation continues: "If you do not know the beauty of fairest among women, if you don't understand the beauty of the soul [the soul here is referred to as a beautiful woman], if you return and haven't reflected in the wisdom before you come here and don't know anything of the mysteries of the upper world, you aren't merited to enter here. Therefore return again. Learn those things that the people consider to be unimportant and know the secrets of the upper world. When you know these secrets of reincarnation, from them shall you learn".

We have all heard the expression, "Out of the mouth of babes comes wisdom", but few really know its meaning. When the Song of Songs[66] instructs us, "and feed thy kids beside the shepherds' tents", it is speaking, the Zohar says,[67] of where the children study. They are only children, but if one listens clearly, he will hear many of the secrets of reincarnation.

Before we conclude this aspect of karma or *tikune*, let us clarify the subject of how a man can be held responsible for the customs and duties of his time. What can be said about a soldier who must, under orders, kill or torture? Why should a man like that be penalized for performing his obligatory or social duty? What about the man who performs an electrocution in a prison — is he personally accountable?

The answer to that seemingly knotty problem is, quite simply, that it depends on your frame of reference. There is an old joke in which someone greets a friend with the standard pleasantry, "How are you?". The perceptive man answers, "Compared to what?".

In Numbers,[68] God commanded Moses to speak to the stone that it might bring forth water, but Moses was angry and he struck the stone. The result was the same, but by that momentary loss of control, he forever surrendered his right to enter the promised land. The observer might legitimately complain that the penalty was monstrous for such a small transgression, and from the observer's frame of reference that would be true. But Moses, who had communed directly with the Creator, lived in a different frame of reference, and only within that framework could his actions be judged.

Someone might say of a previous life, "I was a very pious religious leader". But neither his piety nor his works have meaning outside the frame of reference in which he applied them.

To the unenlightened, an individual might appear to be a veritable saint, yet that same individual might be light years away from fulfilling the *tikune* he bears. Thus when the Talmud[69] tells us, "Judge not your friend until you reach his station", it really is saying that we are incapable of judging until we know the frame of reference within which "your friend" dwells.

In all the universe there is no such thing as an accident. All misfortunes or "accidents" encountered in the present are but the logical outgrowth of some action in a past life or in the present one. Misfortune and illness are merely the effects of causative factors operating under the laws of tikune.

Therefore, anyone who suffers some form of injury or illness should immediately ask himself whether it is the result of a *tikune* condition from a past incarnation or the result of some flaw in the present lifetime. The illness might be nothing more than the result of eating or drinking or smoking too much, but the need some people feel to overindulge invariably has its origin in *tikune*.

From a Kabbalistic standpoint, all forms of pain, suffering, illness and injury have their origins in *tikune* and are there to promote spiritual growth, but *tikune* itself must not be fatalistically interpreted. We cannot escape the results of past actions, but we may change the results by what we do now. If the soul becomes aware of its defects and brings itself into alignment with the forces of the universe, and the cosmic truths of unity, pain and suffering can be modified.

This is not to say that if we encounter a person deep in suffering that we should ignore his cry for help on the grounds that he is merely working off his *tikune*. It is not our duty to interfere with the process, but we can look upon the sufferer in a different light and help him bear his burden without trying to bear it for him. Through imagery and the application of the laws of Kabbalah, we can project ourselves backward in time to see the individual in a different role and by so doing, help him to know the true source of his suffering. In *Ten Luminous Emanations*[70] we read that the soul is part of God and that it is identical with the whole, the Creator, or the universal spirit. The only difference is that the soul is the part and God is the complete universal spirit. Therefore, when we speak of the laws of *tikune*, we must understand that there is a cosmic energy that can help us turn or remove the misfortune that has overcome us.

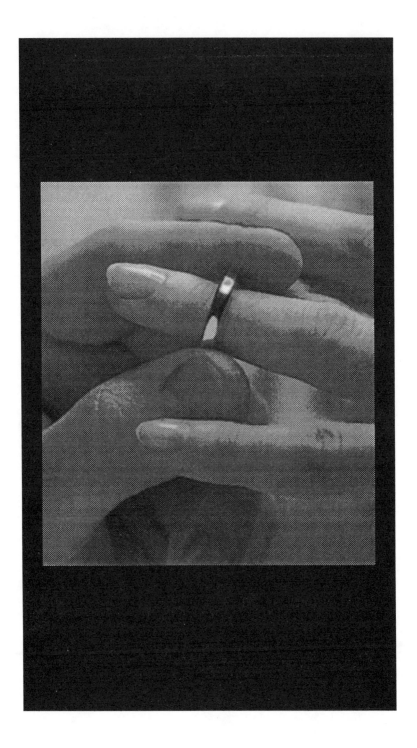

20

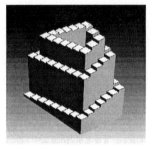

REINCARNATION AND MARRIAGE

FOR SOME NOTHING CAN BE MORE TERRIBLE THAN THE state of marriage. While infinitely rewarding at its best, marriage is unspeakably oppressive at its worst. Marriage offers the utmost extremes of human happiness and human bondage, with all the lesser degrees of felicity and restraint in between.

From the point of view of the law, marriage is a contract, and from the point of view of psychology it might be regarded as a theater of sexual and emotional drama. Jewish traditional law regards it as a sacrament, as does Christian doctrine. The cynic sees it as a trap for fools, saying, quite truthfully, that the best way to kill a romance is to get married.

All of those things may be manifestly true, but according to the enlarged and more comprehensive point of view provided by the reincarnation principle, it would be wrong to accept such truths as total.

Taking all these views together, the expanded point of view reveals marriage as the opportunity for two imperfect individuals to help each other discharge their respective *tikune* debts and advance their spiritual understanding. No marriage is a result of chance and no marriage is begun on a clean slate. Every marriage is but an episode in a series of stories begun long ago in which the parties have been related to each other in previous lives.

In the Zohar[71] it is clearly stated: "Note that all the figures of souls that are to be born stand before the Almighty in pairs". In other words, they are divided into male and female, and eventually, after they have worked their way through the lifetime corridors of reincarnation and have found correction sufficient to merit each other, the Almighty mates them.

There is no bliss in the physical universe greater than that mating. But it must be earned in terms of soul-growth through many lifetimes in which marriage may be anything but bliss.

Soulmates are but two halves — male and female — of what began in the Endless World as a single soul, divided by the hand of the Almighty in preparation for the long trek through this world. Only when tikune is acomplished and karmic debts are discharged can they come together again on this plane, but no marriage is a mistake.

The majority of women accomplish tikune much more swiftly than do their male counterparts and most of them, with exceptions which history occasionally has recorded in savage terms, are here simply to help men bear their karmic burdens. Most women are here on a volunteer basis for the benefit of men with whom they may have endured a number of incarnations. When a woman is seen being especially hard on her husband it usually is an indication that she is doing precisely what she should be doing to help him make his *tikune*.[72]

Scripture tells us there is nothing new under the sun[73] and certainly the wedding of soulmates in any given lifetime is not new since their joining has long since occurred above. They are promised to each other from the beginning. As Rabbi Abba puts it,[74] "happy are the righteous whose souls are beautified before the holy king before they come into this world". When the time comes for soulmates to marry, the Almighty, who knows each spirit and soul, joins them as they were at first and proclaims their union. The male is the aspect of the right column, both of the body and soul, and the female is the aspect of the left co-lumn.

But only if a man has led a virtuous life is he privileged to marry his own true soulmate. The Ari says[75] that there is a time when a female will be reincarnated specifically for the opportunity to marry her soulmate because he may not have had the merit in prior lifetimes to take her.

Even after winning his soulmate, however. a man remains vulnerable. If he then leads an extremely sinful life, he may have to return to this world for the purpose of tikune without his soulmate — a point made clear in the Zohar[76] in Exodus which says, "If he shall enter into slavery by himself, by himself shall he go out".[77] On the surface, this would appear to be but one of several verses dealing with the treatment of slaves, but it actually refers to an individual who has failed, in a given incarnation, to merit union with his soulmate.

Even if the law of *tikune* has freed the female of the need to reincarnate, she may feel so strongly for her soulmate that she may voluntarily return to assist him in his struggle for correction.

It's a wise adage that says' "Marriage is like a besieged fortress — those who are outside want to get in and those who are inside want to get out".

When we look at most marriages, with all the misery they seem to bring to the people involved, it is surprising that anyone would find it a desirable state. When it brings children, it brings with them a veritable horde of heartaches and frustration, yet the unmarried generally have a strong sense of being cheated of something precious in their free but solitary lives.

Some will argue that the sexual aspect of marriage is the key, but that is an argument that will stand up neither from a Kabbalistic-reincarnation point of view nor, in this day of sexual liberation, even as a practical weave in the social fabric. Once, lack of marriage condemned a woman, and in some communities, men as well, to a life of sexual starvation, and past a certain age, a woman automatically became the disesteemed victim of the old maid complex. Today, however, women are free as never before to pursue independent careers and to establish sex lives without fear of censure. With the divorce rate for those who do marry reaching epidemic proportions. Why, then, does anyone bother?

According to the Zohar[78], *tikune*, not biology or social custom is the driving force behind the wedding bells. The Zohar states that "It is marriage that constitutes a difficult task for the Almighty because soulmates — male and female — are two halves of a single soul, split upon creation and sent their separate ways until, through successive incarnations, they have found correction sufficient to merit coming together again on this earth plane. The difficulty lies in the fact that a good man may merit, if not his soulmate, at least a good woman, and that he may find her, only to lose her to her true soulmate, also meriting her, who appears on the scene.

When soulmates meet and marry, knowingly or other-wise, they have agreed to co-star again with one they have known before in one or more lifetimes. The players, at any time, can alter the promise of the plot. The stage has been set, but the lines have not necessarily been written. Yet even if two people are soul-mates, but do not understand the principles of reincarnation, they still may fall prey to problems which, through lack of under-standing, can plunge them unnecessarily into the maelstrom of infidelity and divorce. Many a good marriages goes on the rocks solely through ignorance.

Sociologists and psychologists generally try to explain marital infidelity as a biological phenomenon, but from a kabbal-istic point of view, *tikune* is far more likely to lie at the root of the problem.

Since marriage plays such an important role in any so-ciety, it is important to understand that role. The cosmic laws of reincarnation cannot be changed, and it is lack of knowledge of those laws that spawn so many of today's problems.

In every religion, marriage is proclaimed by a carefully performed ceremony. Even civil marriages require the pronounce-ment of certain lines and the taking of certain vows. Those cere-monies and those vows have served mankind since the beginning of human history, yet increasing numbers of young people today are casting them aside as unimportant.

"We love each other", they say. "We don't need a piece of paper or words mumbled by a third party to prove it".

If they are right about that why are the problems of living

together — married or unmarried — growing in quantum leaps?

The answer is a simple one. Rules and regulations are what make marriage an institution. Abandonment of rules and regulations promotes total disregard for the sanctity of the union between a man and a woman and without the middle column force of that sanctity, short-circuiting becomes almost inevitable.

Such short-circuiting damages far more than the marriage in question. It wreaks havoc on the universe as well because it becomes a primary source of negativity. Many in the ranks of mankind are essentially sitting on the fence. They are neither particularly good nor particularly bad and for them, the balance is easily tipped. An abundance of negativity, created by the short-circuiting that stems from marital strife can lead some people to behave in a negative fashion.

Thus, in addition to the problems of tikune, the individual in the midst of a self-created short circuit finds there is another problem with which to deal. This new problem occurs the moment negativity is added to the cosmic process.

Our objective in any given lifetime is to convert our inherent Desire to Receive into a Desire to Share and only when that has been accomplished do we create a circuit. Thus the purpose of repentance is not simply to say "I'm sorry". It is to restore any positivity to the universe which we might have taken away. As the self is affected, so is the universe affected.

Ritual, therefore, is not empty posturing. It is a metaphysical system under which positive energy is restored.

21

THE MARRIAGE EXERCISE

CONTRARY TO THE DOCTRINE OF SOME RELIGIONS, marriage, once sanctified, is not beyond dissolution. Under biblical doctrine, dissolution is possible but is not to be lightly made.

In the Bible,[79] the institution of divorce is provided for couples who find it beyond their power to live together. The means by which they may be relieved of each other and permitted to go their separate ways to new and better unions, rather than be bound to a lifetime of unhappiness, has existed from the time the Bible was written. But under the institution of divorce, a peacemaking effort must be made. The task of counseling and striving to adjust the grievances of the parties involved is entrusted to the rabbi, and only when all his efforts fail does he permit a divorce to proceed. The system has worked well in the past. Divorce was rare and the Bible's central purpose — which is the preservation of marriage — was largely achieved.

Today, however, with the ceremony and the sanctity of

marriage out of fashion and "meaningful relationships" popular
as a substitute, the pettiest of reasons are given for divorce. No
attempt at compromise and reconcilliation is made. Good will,
perseverance and adaptability are set aside, and with them, the
Bible's purpose in protecting both the marriage and the progeny
which it produces.

No two people have identical tastes or habits. Therefore
when two people live together with all the intimacy that prevails
between a husband and a wife, differences in taste, habit and outlook easily come to the surface, often with disasterous results,
both to themselves and to those who live with and around them.
Yet in most cases, their differences are really trivialities of no consequence.

Such chaff can only be the result of lost spirituality.
When a couple agree on spiritual matters, other differences automatically fade in importance. There can be no bitterness or dissension between a husband and wife who share each other's
ideals.

The laws of marriage, laid down in the past, include the
laws of purity and chastity. Physical and material aspects of marriage have their place, but spiritual claims must come first
because the precious precepts of chastity in family life is what hal-
lows the union of man and woman to assure that their children
will be blessed with purity as well as health. A soul conceived in
the holiness of wedlock will, at the moment of conception, enter
into the fullness of life endowed with the purity that will stand as
the guarantee of his character.

It requires little study of society, with its soul-numbing
atrocities, hatreds, wars and rising crime rates, to discern souls
conceived under other circumstances. For the Zohar[80] teaches

that the thoughts of a man and woman during sexual intercourse are what determines what sort of soul will occupy the body of the baby to be born of their union. When these hallowed claims have been met, the physical expression of marriage may then follow as a sanctified action in which marriage itself becomes a great spiritual force to strengthen the bonds of mutual devotion and loyalty and to assure progeny with a strength of character.

Of necessity, ideas of modesty and morality are inherent in our attitude towards marriage. Without them, marriage is little more than a unity of two individuals who, to outward appearances, love each other, but who may, in reality, fear and hate each other in the depths of their hearts with an intensity which not even they can fathom. Happy is the man whose wife bestows love and faith upon the union and who is to him mother, sister, wife and friend, sharing all his burdens and caring and sustaining the household, even in times of adversity, with love and peace.

Unhappily, these noble and beautiful concepts do not prevail in most marriages and the concept that the traditional home centers always upon a loving wife and a happy man is illusory.

The Ari says[81] if a man can't understand his own soul and the soul of the woman he loves, and if that love is not based on knowledge of reincarnation and deeper understanding, there is no base upon which a marriage can be built. A man must have a true understanding of why he happens to be with the woman in his life. It is within the void created by lack of understanding that today's all too common extramarital relationships are rooted.

In view of all the pain and all the pitfalls that inevitably lie in the path of the best marriages, the miracle is that anyone at all would opt for it. Yet after a decade of disrepute and decline, the institution is finding favor in the United States as never before. Whatever the custom of the day, there is, within the human heart, the innate intuition to seek a spouse. Jewish law states that every man has a duty to marry in order to procreate children. This is spelled out in the Bible:[82] "...And the Almighty blessed them and said unto them, 'be fruitful and multiply and replenish earth!'" Thus, from Genesis onward, the obligation of motherhood has been bestowed upon the woman and that obligation is consistent throughout all sacred literature. It is the primary duty for which she was formed. Thus, when Adam named his partner, he called her Hava [Eve] because she was the mother of all Hai [living].[83] According to the Zohar,[84] names always signify the major functions in creation of those who bear them. Hence Eve's name contains within it the function for which she was created.

The Bible emphasizes the importance of procreation throughout. Sarah's unhappiness at being barren gives way to happiness when Isaac is born to her.[85] Rebekah, in preparing for marriage, receives the blessing that she will have issue.[86] Rachel voices pure misery when she says to Jacob, "Give me children or else I will die".[87] David sings, "Thy wife shall be as fruitful as a fruitful vine".[88] With such an underpinning, marriage has always been considered a divinely ordained institution in which the duty of procreation may become fulfilled.

There is always more to the Bible than first meets the eye. Essentially, it is written in a code for which the Kabbalah is the key. As the Zohar puts it, "Those who consider the stories of the Torah to indicate merely a story alone are foolish and uninformed, for if that were the case, then the supernal Torah, which is full of holiness and truth, could have been written by anyone who was qualified to write beautiful stories".[89] The Bible is filled with stories of lust and perversion — Tamar, Yehudah the son of

Jacob, Lot and his daughters[90] — but because the Bible is more than just a television script going no farther than the story line, these accounts must be read and understood at a far deeper level than is generally accepted. It is incumbent upon us to understand the inner mystical meaning of the Bible in connection with marriage and procreation. Biblical precepts that guard the purity of marriage are a strong factor in creating a solid mutual relationship between husband and wife, and in assuring that children born of such a union will bear its imprint throughout their lives. We cannot, however, hide the instability and lack of devotion that mars most modern marriages. We must come to grips with the reality of today — a reality that has made the noble words of our sages ring empty and hollow. If we are to return to the beautiful aspects of marriage, a thorough understanding of reincarnation is necessary.

"וַיּוָלֵד...
וַיִּקְרָא
אֶת שְׁמוֹ..."

(בְּרֵאשִׁית ה')

22

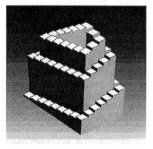

REINCARNATION AND GIVEN NAMES

A KEY FACTOR IN ACHIEVING CONTROL OF OUR LIVES lies in the individual's given name. Surnames are of no importance. They are worn and discarded like so many suits of clothes in the course of many incarnations, but the given name never changes. It is chosen to correspond with the soul. Parents should always name their children after relatives or loved ones, who were giving people, with whom they felt a soul affinity. They really have no choice beyond selecting the name the child brings into the world from past incarnations. They may think they have chosen, but in reality, they have not.

Thus, to name a child after someone other than a loved one is frequently to set that child at odds with his own identity — especially if the namesake has died in a particularly violent or bizarre manner. His name can burden the child with a remnant of the *tikune* he was working out at his death. Frequently, a parent will come to me with a tale of woe regarding trouble he is having with a son or a daughter. My first question, always, is, "who was the child named after?" In virtually every case, the "trouble" will prove to be less with the child than with the namesake whose particular vices the child is reflecting.

There have been periods of history — both among jews and non-Jews — when Biblical names have been in vogue. There you will find Christians named Joshua or Adam or Enoch. Then, inexplicably, the popularity of Biblical names yields to more secular names. The Kabbalistic explanation is that Biblical names prevail in periods of great revealment and enlightenment while retreat from them will come as darkness descends over the human spirit. Above all names, those selected from the Bible are constructed by letters that are vehicles of energy transfer, and the Bible holds a specific verse for every one of them and he who meditates upon his own verse will find himself at the threshold of the time tunnel that leads back to memory of previous incarnations when his body and his circumstances were different, but his name, essentially, was the same.[91]

Names can be the same across language barriers. Joseph becomes Jose in Spanish and Giuseppe in Italian with no change of essence unless it is corrupted into a diminutive or a nickname. Both should be avoided simply because both represent distortions of the vehicle.

So powerful is the influence of a name, and so powerful is the negativity surrounding the wrong name, that a Kabbalistic answer for great physical or spiritual illness frequently is a name change in an effort to steer the individual back to connection with his true identity. Like any technique, it is not foolproof, but virtually every case of conflict within an individual personality can be traced to an improperly assigned name.

Such a practical application can be illustrated by the case

of a young man who was enrolled in one of my reincarnation classes. His son had been born with a birth defect which left him with no muscular support in the right side of his neck. The child's head leaned, as a result, constantly to the right. In search of a cause for this affliction, we plunged into a discussion of the father's family background and he revealed that his sister had been murdered before the birth of the afflicted child. The murder weapon was a gun and the fatal bullet had ripped through the right side of her neck. Though the child in question was a boy, his given name was similar to that of his father's sister.

That the child could have been the reincarnation of the man's sister was an obvious conclusion and one that could have been prevented had the man and his wife been able to understand and apply the principles of reincarnation when the child was conceived.

As this example will show, the immediate application of knowledge of reincarnation lies in the area of problem solving. In the face of any affliction — emotional or mental — it will take its practitioner below the level of consciousness where the causes of visible effects lie buried. To approach such problems without making that journey is like trying to fight crabgrass with a lawnmower.

Through knowledge of reincarnation, an individual can probe not only into the immediate causes of his problems, but into the causes of the causes as well. The technique of reincarnation will enable its practitioner to dig deeply into his own ingrained attitudes and expectations to better his chances of benefitting from the knowledge he has acquired. The extent to which the individual uses such knowledge to overcome the things that bedevil him is, of course, entirely a matter of choice. Some may be content to gain one small glimmer of illumination while others aim at nothing less than liberation from the relentless spinning wheel of repeated embodiments. But for all who gain it, the ability to recollect former existences will lead to less materialistic modes of thought and enhance the appreciation of spirituality in mind and soul.

Knowledge of reincarnation and of Kabbalistic meditation techniques therefore are among the most pragmatic of approaches to life.

One who is in great economic distress may find respite and an understanding of his problems and their cure through many retro-trips in which he can re-experience the more pleasurable and affluent periods in prior lifetimes. The depressed may re-experience hope, the grieving find solace and the imprisoned thrill to freedom. One never is too poor or too pressed for time to open up the wonders of the world and call upon the powers of creative visualization. Kabbalistic meditation produces a high without drugs or alcohol and, more importantly, it will be followed by an afterglow rather than by a hangover. It has the power to abolish all the ancient fears of death, poverty, illness, rejection and loneliness that have, for too long, overshadowed human thinking.

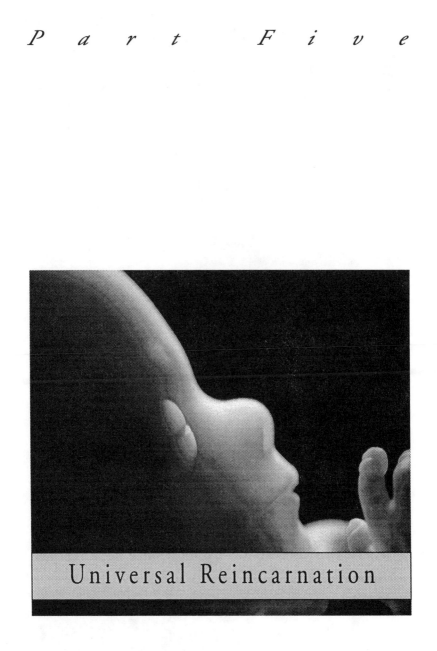

Universal Reincarnation

23

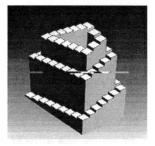

GLOBAL INCARNATION

WHY DO SOME NATIONS FLOUNDER AND OTHERS FLOURISH? Why do some nations continue to get richer while others stagnate financially to the point of economic disaster? Why have certain segments of the globe experienced incredible scientific development, whereas others have not, or even in some cases have retrogressed to the point of oblivion? Why could Japan, after 1970 and not earlier, jump into and join with the industrialized nations of the world so rapidly, and yet neighboring China retain a pattern of development that was clearly stagnated? Why did Russia continue to become a world power after World War II, while England, "over whose flag the sun never set", during the same period failed to progress or develop? Why have world empires after an illustrious reign of majestic power lapsed into a state of non-existence, passing briefly, as the wind, across the stage of history?

The question of why some societies progressed and others did not, is one of the most puzzling and difficult facing the historian and his interpretation of global and human history. The famous historian Joseph Needham, (after whom this mystery has sometimes been referred to as the "Needham problem"), after having written many books on the subject, still confesses that he really doesn't know the answer.

Global and human interaction which takes place in modern society combined with some very complex relationships and significant changes in our environment — dramatic climatic changes, nuclear explosions — make it just about impossible to identify the reason or reasons for the different patterns of progress or regression in different societies. Why do some think of things that others haven't thought of? The thought process which is so profound and enormous, going on subconsciously in the human brain, suddenly appears among the people of certain parts of the globe, while human beings who seem to be dull and boring appear in other sections of our terrestrial planet.

In essence we are faced with two basic dilemmas. Firstly, why the human brain develops new ideas, new discoveries or philosophies in some and not others is a question dealt with in another chapter of this book. What concerns us here is the primal cause of the particular development patterns of different societies. It has been suggested that a society which is intolerant of criticism, suppressing all forms of dissent and maintaining a social order of rigid orthodoxy may possibly account for stagnation. One where tolerance of new ideas or radical dissension is permitted will result in a considerable increase in its capacity for innovation. This principle along with many others that have been proposed, continue to circumvent the principle of cause and effect. The fallacy in this type of reason lies precisely in the fact that what is cause and what is effect has never been determined. Which comes first, the chicken or the egg? Tolerance or the lack thereof in any given society may, in effect, be merely the result of a progressive society, rather than the cause of it.

From a Kabbalistic point of view of reality, one question must be raised and that is, "what caused what in the first place"? Some societies which are tolerant of dissent experience technological advances. Is tolerance the primal cause? Might this be the other way around? What determines what, is very hard to say. We seem to know little concerning primal cause, and this is precisely the reason why so much has been written and suggested on this subject with very few, if any, final answers.

I have stressed from time to time the need for a complete reorientation of our analytical process. The Kabbalistic world view of our universe holds out great promise towards a single coherent picture of reality. It implies that when seeking the true primal causes of physical events, we must take virtually the whole universe into account, even when this necessitates the acknowledgement of instantaneous responses of particles or intelligent cosmic energy to each other's actions, although separated by distances across our universe. While this kind of acceptance of instant, immediate interaction violates the principles of the relativity theory's opposition to quicker-than-light velocities, nevertheless, the scientist is and continues to be confounded by the ever-changing phenomena of reality. Consequently, the Kabbalistic attempt to provide a complete picture of reality on the level of metaphysics is a most welcome fountain for universal information where results of different experiments of our cosmic whole can and will fit into a single coherent interface of paradoxical quantum mechanics. The baffling holism of interdependence raised by the quantum theory need not lead us to an outright rejection of quantum phenomena. Rather, its implications point to the faster-than light connection in which cosmic intelligences may indeed provide measuring devices and techniques by which science will correlate and connect states of spatially separated entities. The comprehensibility of our universe need not remain an eternal mystery.

To find out what this cosmic intelligent energy is and to learn more about this strange phenomenon, and how global interaction and incarnation are manipulated by its awesome force, let us turn to the source, the *Sefer Yetzira*, the Book of Formation. The sometimes unpleasant symptoms of the sub-atomic level of energy to a physicist or sudden space changes for an astronaut can be unsettling. This is precisely why Kabbalistic information is just beginning to be understood, and will hopeful-ly place the law of cause and effect in its proper perspective. The new age of thought seems to be reuniting with the Kabbalistic view of the structure of energy or, as I like to refer to it, the uni-versal cosmic currency of human consciousness.

> Rabbi Judah discoursed on the verse: "And the Lord said, Let there be a firmament in the midst of the waters"[92] "When the Lord created the world", he said, "He created seven firmaments above, and in each one stars and constellations and ministers to serve ... . Similarly, there are seven earths below, one spiritually higher [in ener-gy] than the other, the Land of Israel being the highest of all and Jerusalem being the energy cen-ter in the whole inhabited world. Our colleagues who dwell in the South have seen all this in the books of the ancients and in the Book of Adam. The lands of earth are all divided as the firma-ment [Van Allen Belts] above which divide one from another ... . The creatures in them are also different, ... and their aspects also differ. But, it may be asked, are not all men descended from Adam, and did not Adam go down to each of

these earths and beget sons there? The truth is, however, that man is found only in this highest earth which is called *Tevel* (inhabited world), which is attached to the upper firmament and to the Supreme Source, the Force. Hence man is superior to all other creatures. For, just as above there exists the highest firmament which is the throne of the Lord, the Force, so below on this *Tevel* is the manifestor and king of all, to wit, man. As for the lower creatures, they are produced from the moisture of the earth along with an influence of the Force from above which produces creatures of various kinds, some with skins and some with shells — as the worm creatures in the earth — red, black or white and other colors — their life span enduring no more than ten years. In the Book of Reb Hamnuna the Elder it is further explained that all the inhabited world is like a ball, so that some are above and some below, and the appearances of certain races around the world so that some are affected by the Force as above, some races are affected more than others by the Force. Similarly, the division of earth's ball is divided into seven major segments referred to as the seven lands. The different appearances of the inhabited world is directly dependent upon the difference of the cosmic air (atmosphere) that exists in each segment. Therefore, the cosmic Force makes manifest that there is a part of the ball of earth where it is light when in another part of the earth it is dark. Therefore some have night while others have day. Also there is a place where it is always day and where there is no night save for a very short time.

This account of the universal structure and different cosmic atmospheres is to be found in the books of the ancients and in the Book of Adam. There are principally seven universes and these seven universes are separated from each other by seven cosmic atmospheres. This mystery has been entrusted to the masters of the Kabbalah, but it is not known to those who mark out boundaries, the geographers."[93]

Now and then a scientist stumbles across a fact that seems to solve one of the great mysteries of our civilization. Such unexpected discoveries are usually rare and far in between. However, when they do occur, it usually fails to explain those rudimentary, fundamental evolutionary precepts that have hardly changed at all throughout history.

But, one may ask, hasn't change become an integral part of our way of life? In contrast, human behavior, the power and force behind dramatic changes in our lifestyle have not undergone the process of change. War, hate, love and other familiar characteristics of humankind seem to be little affected by environmental changes constantly taking place all around us. The big question is, what is this Force that can control the psyche of man and yet at the same time permit the extraordinary outburst of major inventions and breakthroughs? What is the catalyst behind the remarkable outpouring of new technology in the past few years? What accounts for the innovative adaptiveness and inventiveness in early America — like the telegraph, cotton gin, steamboat and more recently in high-technology?

Similarly there are seven earths below, one spiritually higher in energy than the other .... The creatures in them are also different.

The startling revelation that creatures are different because of spiritually infused energy of different gradations by the Force, accounts, in great measure for the different and also more innovative psyche of its inhabitants along with its natural resources. The basic building blocks for both come from the same awesome source, the Cosmic Force, which becomes manifest in seven orbiting structures, the seven planets. The idea that the Force radiates energy through the sun within the solar system is not new.

Why are planetary probes or artificial satellites equipped with solar energy systems? The first small space station is also designed to use the sun's energy more efficiently. From a Kabbalistic world view of our universe, we merely reflect inward, no less than the physicist probing further inward towards the elusive world of subatomic phenomena. Rather than taking the sun as the primal force of energy, the Zoharic point of view states that all manifested forms of energy are merely the result of natural, intelligent cosmic emissions that ultimately become clothed in orbital channels. These cosmic beacons all originate in the Force and become varied as they pass through varied terrestrial orbital channels. Consequently, it may come as no surprise when these cosmic intelligences are detected, and seen as messengers from the Force, seeding earth with complex organic intelligent forms. These encapsulated intelligent coded messages, known as *Sfirot* or metaphysical DNA, are the primal forces that account for our grand solar system and for earth's cosmic division. In this scenario, earth has produced a network of societies that ultimately appear in various regions providing the cultural birthright of every race with its specific science, intelligence, art and history. One day, some of humankind's most talented minds might decode these interstellar messages and discover the intelligent civilizations of outer space, civilizations which are and have been known by the Kabbalist. In a word, these extraterrestrial messages are the complex forms of Sfirot which encapsulate the Force.

What seems to emerge from the Zohar, is that seven forms of intelligence which emanate from the seven *Sfirot*[94] are directly responsible for our universal manifestation. These advanced extraterrestrial non-corporeal beings living in a solar system similar to ours direct the orbiting structures of our own universe and subsequently display the various quantified degrees of the Force in varied and specific sections of our planet earth.

All life dances to the music of astral influences as more clearly demonstrated by cyclical phenomena. Unseen extra terrestrial forces affect terrestrial affairs and decidedly determine the ups and downs of many phenomena related to mankind. By tracking the cycles of ups and downs of terrestrial life and identifying these cycles, the curious fluctuations clearly suggest a metaphysical pattern very closely resembling what DNA is to us. While enormous research has been undertaken in the past few decades to investigate cycles, the mystery as to what causes it remains at the core of scientific frustration. However, were the scientific communities amenable to accepting the hypothesis that terrestrial activity is subject to celestial cosmic influence, as so clearly stated in the Zohar, much of scientific data, now shrouded in mystery, might just open up endless new frontiers in nature never before imagined. Physical forces that obey acceptable scientific law, from a Kabbalistic world view, rest with and depend upon cosmic intelligent forces.

Consequently, the seven planes, acting as orbital channels for the seven diffused forms and levels of cosmic intelligence known as the seven *Sfirot* — according to the Zohar — mark their celestial imprint on the face of earth. It is a non-material force. This force has an intelligence of its own. It might be compared to the soul of man which makes each individual distinctively different from any other. The soul is responsible for a person's creativity, free will or emotions such as love, hate, fear and warring instincts. The seven non-material entities cause the individual diversity of the universe and earth. The division of earth is, therefore, directly related to the aspect of intelligence that inhabits a particular section or country. This force controls its inhabitants the same way a programmer directs a computer or a pilot maneuvers an airplane. The particular level of intelligence is responsible for the particular division of our earth. The inhabitant of Germany is not under the same cosmic influence as, say, one living in Russia. Traits and customs which are characteristic of one nation cannot and are not similar to any other. These differences are the direct result of each nation's peculiar cosmic influence.

Does this revelation then imply that all people of one nation act and behave alike? Of course not! People remain individuals. Then how do we reconcile the establishment of common traits and customs of a nation due to its particular cosmic energy infusion and the ability of each person to maintain his own individual and unique characteristics?

A similar mystery that I would like to explore is the conflict between continuous change and man's stubborn insistence to cling to well defined modes of behavior. The inevitable process of change that has become a by-word in high technology makes us wonder how life forms still hang on unchanged for so long a time. In a quickening evolutionary society, humankind as well as all other life forms maintain their desires for the very same things that our forefathers did. Startling breakthroughs that ultimately foster the biggest leaps have had very little effect on human thinking. Conservative stability still seems to be the rule for most species within our universe. Is our frame of mind really different from that of the people of the Middle Ages? In spite of dramatic environmental changes along with the progress syndrome, have human psychological needs really changed down through the centuries? It remains crystal clear that we still retain our primal and primitive characteristics which have indeed permitted us to cope with life's hardships. Do we really better ourselves by growing with progress which continues to become more complex with passing time? Does this mean that we are to regard lack of change as an evolutionary failure?

Indeed, no mystery in the long history of our universe is so startling as the universal and repeated behavior of its inhabitants. So little is this subject understood that we need not marvel at our continued insistence on destroying each other. If we must marvel, let it be at our own inability to unlock the secrets of human behavioral patterns. The study of split global or national society patterns is a field in turmoil. It is a field where we find experts in disagreement on virtually every point. The only fact now generally accepted is the need for additional pathways that focus more attention on the subtle, internal level of things, and yet meets the most rigorous demands of science.

Fundamental evolutionary precepts have hardly changed at all throughout history. We have witnessed civilizations weave through the fiber of recorded history, attempting to impose their kind of order. This, a kind of mastery over man's environment, persists and remains as part of the world picture. Consequently, when we come across information that can bridge the gap between the two aspects of our society, it is really exciting, and what's more, refreshing. We therefore turn again to the Zohar in our attempt to throw some light upon sociological and psychological questions that have been raised.

Rabbi Shimon here introduced the subject of transmigration of souls, saying: Onkelos translates

the above words as follows: These are the judgments which thou shalt order before them. In
other words, These are the orders of the
metempsychosis; the judgments of the souls, by
which each of them receives its appropriate punishments. Associates, the time is now arrived to
reveal diverse hidden and secret mysteries in
regard to the transmigration of souls."[95].

Reincarnation is not a thing of the past. The Ari, R. Isaac
Luria, tells us that at the time of the Aquarian age souls of the
Exodus generation shall again be incarnated[96].

Hence, the story of our universe is really a story of returning souls. Precisely what accounts for the uninterrupted
unchanged evolutionary process of mankind? Whether or not we
fully understand what draws a soul's entrance into the present
plane, it is vital to know that we have all been here before. Thus,
when considering man's behavioral patterns, we are in essence
seeing aspects of ourselves in former lifetimes. Life for most of us
is almost a re-run of our activities as experienced back in *tikune*
and some task we attempted before but somehow failed. It is precisely for this reason that man remains in an unalterable psychological state of mind. Consequently, man still maintains his primal characteristics and clings to well-defined modes of existence, inasmuch as man in the twentieth century is a mini
motion picture over and over again. What seems to emerge
from the Kabbalistic view and what I am suggesting is that
human behavior is not only genetically controlled to a significant degree, but that, additionally, the *Tikune* process directs
and dictates the traits of modern man as well as the patterns of
love, hate and aggression exhibited today. Now I know that this
position challenges the conventional view of most social scientists who claim that cultural and environmental upbringing and

not incarnation or biologically related imperatives shape human nature. The far-ranging effects of our internal human spirit extend through our characteristics whether one lives in a city or rural community.

The external behavior such as traits and customs are fully determined by the cosmic force prevailing in a particular part of the globe. If we could turn inward, to the human range of spirit, we would have an almost unlimited scope for answers of earth's complexities. Consequently, the evolution of an individual's bigotry and racism, for example, would not stem from present interactions and associations with other groups. Only a greater understanding of the *Tikune* process will free man from bigotry and racism. Environmental influences do not promote behavioral or physical differences between people. The returning souls leave us with our passions and petty hatreds. Rebellion against authority, women's liberation and abandonment of religion are all traits that have seen their faces once before on the stage of history. These deep seated innate tendencies transcend the peculiar cosmic influence of a section of our globe. This, then, accounts for why some nations get richer while others stagnate to the point of economic disaster. Why some societies progress and others do not can be seen as a relationship between the specific area on earth and its cosmic connection to the cosmic force. A society which is intolerant of criticism, maintaining a social order or rigid orthodoxy is a result of the specific cosmic force regulating its social order, and is not to be considered a cause for its social conduct. Simplistic theories of genetic determinism cannot be used to explain or justify racial hatred and oppression as in the case of Nazi Germany. One may then raise a serious, and certainly thorny question! Does this imply that Nazism was cosmically regulated? And consequently, should those who participated in the holocaust be considered the perpetrators of the crimes committed?

The global astral forces deal with and are more closely aligned with the physical, external behavior that stretches across our globe. They determine the natural resources that appear in one place and not another. They govern the metaphysical data processing information, where externalization, the physical expressions of custom and traits become the habitat for souls who, for reasons of the *Tikune* process, will locate in one particular section over another. These distinct characteristics define the soul's physical expression, and hence, the area of pursuit in the *Tikune* process. Consequently, matters that relate to the exterior culture of any nation will depend upon the particular cosmic force governing the area. Cold rational scientific materialization will depend upon the extent and intensity of the "Desire to Receive" of a specific astral influence generating these cosmic forces. Scientific development or the lack thereof depends on the Desire to Receive. What is a flourishing nation if not its Desire to Receive majestic power? Why does a nation retain a pattern of high-technology, if not for the purpose of achieving ultimate domination and supremacy as a world power?

It is precisely here where the distinction between global cosmic influence and man's free will and his innate love of sharing is keenly felt. The criminals against humanity were placed within the particular frame of reference of cosmic negativity that prevailed over Germany. These were the same individuals returning incarnated according to their earlier failure in the *Tikune* process. They were now faced with a similar challenge of either exercising free will and thwarting the cosmic force of extreme negativity or succumbing to its influence.

We might ask at this time, is this really fair? The answer lies precisely in the purpose for creation at its very inception[97], namely the removal of "Bread of Shame". These negative frames of reference provide man with an opportunity to exercise free will and thus achieve the removal of Bread of Shame. Obviously, if these negative cosmic forces did not exist, then man would simply conform to a preprogrammed kind of intelligence that dictates the sharing philosophy and leave little room for our destructive passions, hatreds and other contemptible traits that distinguish us from computers. Therefore, while on the one hand cosmic negativity aroused and triggered odious behavior within the framework of Nazi Germany, this influence, as powerful as it was, could have and should have been regulated and controlled. This is the obligation and purpose of freethinking and free-choosing mankind.

Our ability to study the universe has been primarily dependent on information received in visible light. To advance our understanding of the material universe in which we live, there is a necessity to begin observing its intrinsic internal dynamics.

> JERUSALEM THE ENERGY CENTER OF THE WORLD
> Similarly there are seven earths below one higher than the other, the Land of Israel being the highest of all and Jerusalem being the highest (center of energy) point in the whole inhabited world.[98]

This is not the first time the Zohar indicates the enormous power that seems to be located within the energy center of Israel.

> It says in the Book of R. Hamnuna the Elder, in connection with the words, "Now there arose a new king over Egypt", that all nations of the world, past, present, and future and all their kings become powerful only on account of Israel. Egypt, for instance did not rule over the whole

world before Israel settled there. The same is true of Babylon (586 B.C.E.), Greece (200 B.C.E.) as well as Edom (Rome 60 B.C.E.). Before that all these nations were utterly insignificant and contemptible. It was entirely due to Israel that they became great.[99]

The truth of these words of the Zohar becomes strikingly clear if we consider for a moment the fate of the land of Israel in relation to the course of history of other nations of the world. Thus we find the Parthian empire of Cyrus reaching its peak at a time when Jews were living in exile in that country. A similar phenomenon occurs in the case of the Babylonian, Greek and Roman empires, and, more recently, in the Ottoman empire. The most recent example of this extraordinary pattern is the British empire. In each case, the country in question reached the peak of its international influence at the time when it ruled over the land of Israel, and measured its decline from the time when it lost possession of that Land.

When patterns begin forming, we should consider the metaphysical force or forces behind them. The Zohar reveals the existence of these internal cosmic forces that shape the history of our universe. On its description of Israel, one cannot but take notice of the interconnectedness between former world powers and Israel's intrinsic energy center. This is precisely the reason why nations have sought to tap its energy resources. However, cautions the Zohar, this mysterious awesome cosmic powerhouse that turns the universe can also heap destruction on those unfamiliar with or lack the proper bond for cosmic connection. Thus, we are provided with yet another example of earth's atmospheric influence over humankind's destiny. Providing an incarnated soul with an environment that meets the specifications of the *Tikune* process will result in some souls appearing in a particular part of the globe, so as to fulfill their *Tikune.*

Consequently, when we raised the question as to why things happen as they do in one area and not another, we see that the people making history were destined to return to where they did, exerting astral influences on earth as an integral part of the whole world of reincarnation.

24

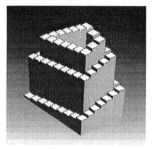

ATLANTIS

MANKIND AND ITS CIVILIZATIONS, LIKE THOSE OF US TODAY, have been born, made their imprint known, and will all eventually die. This procedure will continue to be manifest until the final curtain on the age of Aquarius comes down.

In recent years we have witnessed the first great achievements in radio astronomy and the dawn of the space age. Although man knows that he has lived on this planet for many years, the biblical recorded history is about all we have in the way of written documents.

Even these five thousand years are not sufficiently well known.

Most of us are familiar with the story of the island of Atlantis as narrated by Plato. The island of Atlantis ruled Africa as far as the border of Egypt and Europe to Tuscany on the Apennine peninsula.

Then one fatal evening the island was destroyed by earthquakes and other natural disturbances. It sank into the ocean and vanished, never to be heard from again. According to the story, the inhabitants of this island had reached a highly sophisticated level of conscious development. Attaining this degree of cosmic consciousness they achieved full control of energy fields and their environment. There were among them, unfortunately, those who made an attempt to make use of this enormous power to enslave others. A struggle then developed between them, resulting in the eventual destruction of their land.

Earthquakes and other forms of disaster were the direct result of an internal clash between good and evil which wrought this disaster. The survivors who managed to reach other lands took an oath that never again would this knowledge be revealed to the public. The secrets of cosmic and solar energy would remain for the select few. Aspirants would have to demonstrate, through their piety, their ability to correctly make use of this secret knowledge long before the teaching would become available. Then, and only then, when the student was ready, would the master appear. The eligible ones were furnished with information depending upon their level of spirituality in which they were prepared to make use of it "not for themselves alone". Having sustained a level of elevated consciousness they then became the recipients of this knowledge that was not available to the average person.

The story never ceases to occupy the imagination of learned people. While many thought and still think, that the tale of Atlantis was a figment of Plato's imagination, even to the present the tradition as described by Plato persists and refuses to die. There just doesn't seem to be an appropriate closet in which the story could simply fade away.

Poets and fiction writers have exploited the tale freely: men of science have done this with caution. In the latter part of the nineteenth century, expeditions set out over the Atlantic ocean in search of Atlantis. Recently, prior to World War II, there were societies created for the purpose of investigating the phenomenon of the sunken island. While much speculation has been offered as to its whereabouts, the research and discussions concerning the cultural and scientific achievements seem to be far more interesting.

Were there really former civilizations equal to or more advanced in information sciences than our own? Unfortunately, or fortunately, we consider our age as the most enlightened and sophisticated in all of history, and the story of Atlantis a myth. I say fortunately simply for the reason that a great deal of non-existent theory has been prevented from entering the walls of scientific research. The biblical Deluge seems to have affected every known culture on earth. The great libraries of the past represented man's attempts to salvage everything possible that would provide some clues of former civilizations that seemed to have vanished into thin air.

Even by our own standards, the tremendous size and vastness of the library of Alexandria is incredible. Created in 330 B.C. in honor of Alexander the Great, Alexandria was the Capital of the Ptolemies for some 300 years. As the largest city in the then known world of the west, Alexandria flattered itself with two enormous libraries containing about 700,000 rare books. After the deluge and other global catastrophes, surviving scholars always undertook the task of restructuring history, documenting human wisdom of the past and the preservation of knowledge. The achievements were virtually destroyed when Julius Caesar himself burned this great library to the ground, forever sealing the plethora of important material.

The incredible collection of Psistratus in Athens suffered a similar fate. All that remained for us today were the poems of Homer. Carthage, an ancient city in north Africa founded by the Phoenicians near the site of modern Tunis, saw its grandiose library which housed over half a million volumes destroyed by the Roman Legions in 146 B.C.

There must have been an enormous amount of information gathered through archaeological probing of previous eras. Ironically, the Bible along with the Book of Splendor has and is still not regarded as a source of reliable historical information.

Much of man's antediluvian material seems to have been permanently destroyed or disappeared. However, the Bible stubbornly persists to be a source of historical development and refuses to fade away. The Scroll, in whatever part of the world it may find itself, retains its originality. Furthermore, subscribing the Halakhic point of view, even so much as one incorrect letter invalidated the entire use thereof.[100] This, in my opinion, is precisely the reason why the Bible should be considered a wellspring for antediluvian information. Maybe this seems to be the reason for its neglect! Its authenticity is too exact and detailed. Science is still floundering in its efforts to reconstruct the past.

From a biblical point of view, there is no study which appeals more strongly to the imagination of the individual than that of the peoples of the great deluge and the generation of the tower of Babel. Returning to our question as to whether former civilizations were equally or possibly more advanced in information sciences. Let us turn to the biblical passage concerning the tower of Babel.[101]

And the whole earth was of one language (Hebrew) and of one speech. And it came to pass, as they journeyed *miqedem* (eastward), that they found a plain in the land of Shinar, and they dwelt there.

The Zohar[102] discussed the verse as follows:

The term *miqedem* signifies away from the source of the world. "That they found". We should have expected "saw"; but the word found is used to indicate that they found remnants of the secret wisdom that had been left by the generation of the flood and with that they made their attempt to provoke the source. As they said, so they did. Note what is written, "Behold they are one people and they have all one language. Being of one mind, of one will, and speaking one language, nothing will be withholden from them, which they purpose to do"... the supernal judgment was powerless against them. ... Rabbi Jose said: From here we learn that quarrelsome people soon come to grief, for we see here that as long as the peoples of the world lived in harmony, being of one mind and one will, although they rebelled against the source, the supernal judgment could not touch them, but as soon as they were divided, "the Lord scattered them abroad."

The tales of the great deluge and the Tower of Babel brought overwhelming destruction to the entire world. That of the deluge was most devastating. Water covered the land and annihilated the inhabitants of earth, erasing every memory of what had happened up to that time. Furthermore, the secret wisdom mentioned in the Zohar which was the awesome power of former advanced civilizations, disappeared along with the flood.

Nevertheless the catastrophic deluge did not prevent golden ages of civilization or science to reappear. The ruins of many advanced civilizations speak for themselves. The Memphis constructed by Menes, the Temple of Karnak, and other wonders of the world are testimonial to the degree of technology that once existed.

The civilization of the Babel era was witness to real science born in the remotest periods of antiquity. They managed to salvage only fragments of the language. Advanced civilizations, tremendously different and in most cases greater than our own, have existed in past history as recorded by the oldest and most reliable source of recorded history, the Bible. It was eclipsed by the Lord confounding their language[103] and again reestablished with the demise of the Middle Kingdom of Egypt and the great Exodus. It reached its summit during the period of the first and second Temples when it came into vogue once more The destruction of the second Temple brought with it the disappearance of this awesome power. Its appearance and development would have to wait for the age of Aquarius.[104]

Where did this knowledge of ancient man originate? Where is it today? While modern historians reject the idea that ancient man possessed wide and advanced knowledge there is much evidence to indicate that great technological advancements did exist during remote ancient times.

The Biblical deluge seems to have affected every known culture on earth. How, then, did man of old acquire this knowledge of power? "This is the book of generations of Adam". We find stated in the Zohar as follows:[105] "Rabbi Abba said: The Lord did indeed send down a book to Adam from which he became acquainted with the supernal wisdom of the Power Source. It came later into the hands of the "sons of the Lord"[106], the wise of their generation. Whoever was privileged to peruse it could learn from the awesome power of the Source and its wisdom. This book was brought down to Adam by the master of mysteries, the Angel, Raziel.

Three angels always accompanied and kept watch over the book so as to prevent its falling into improper hands. When Adam was expelled from the garden of Eden he tried to keep hold of this book, but it flew out of his hands. He therefore prayed to the Lord with tears for its return.

It was given back to him in order that the wisdom might not be forgotten by men and that they might strive to obtain knowledge of the Creator by understanding the Power Source, The Light. We also learnt that Enoch had the book which became known as the *"Book of Enoch"*.[107] When the Lord took Enoch he showed him all the supernal mysteries and the Tree of Life in the midst of the garden of Eden. Enoch passes on the knowledge to those ready to accept it plus all of the leaves and branches of the Tree of Life.

Happy are those of exalted spiritual piety to whom the wisdom has been revealed and from whom it will never be forgotten. So states the scripture: "The secret of the Lord is with them that fear Him and his secret to make them know it".[108]

This then was the fount which spiritual man could draw from to fill his thirst for knowledge, wisdom and power. The idea that during the Golden Age of Rabbi Shimon bar Yohai and before these Sages knew and possessed knowledge of the entire earth and all its inhabitants is clearly demonstrated in the Zohar.[109]

In the book of Rabbi Hamnuna the Elder it is

explained further that all the inhabited world is circular like a ball so that some are above and some are below.

Considerable speculation has been offered as to the whereabouts of not only Atlantis itself, but also the advanced knowledge of its inhabitants. Where did the idea of Atlantis originate, if indeed there did exist an Atlantis at all? In fact, Strabo and Pliny were both of the opinion that the tale of Atlantis was an illusion of Plato. Plato himself had no access to any literary works that might have shed some light on the matter. Unfortunately, knowledge of previous civilizations and their learned men perished by fire or catastrophes. All Plato could and did do was to record the story heard two generations before from the wise ruler of Athens, Solon.[110] Solon on a visit to the high Priests of Egypt heard the following story:

> The ocean that was there at that time was navigable. For in the front of its mouth (we might understand this to mean Gibraltar) which you Greeks call the Pillars of Heracles, there lay an island which was larger than Lybia and Asia together. It was possible for the travellers of that time to cross from it to other islands, and from the islands onward to the whole of the continent over against them which encompasses that ocean. Beyond is a real ocean, and the land surrounding it may be considered a continent. In this Island of Atlantis existed a confederation of kings a great and marvelous power, which held sway over all the island and many other lands.

This was Plato's story. The priest told Solon that one day this mighty kingdom on Atlantis near the (Atlantic) Ocean submerged and sank forever into the water. What of its inhabitants? Did they merely just drown, or did their advanced information remain alive?

Unfortunately, Atlantis is a bit vain and is unwilling to reveal her presence. Novelists and poets are persistent, and I will therefore make an attempt to tell you something of its existence and the nature of the people who inhabited her.

"For whenever the Lord allowed the deep mysteries of wisdom to be brought down into the world, mankind was corrupted by them and attempted to declare war on the Source, The Holy One. He gave supernal wisdom to Adam, but Adam utilized the wisdom disclosed to him to familiarize and attach himself to the *yetzer-hara*, evil inclination. and the fountains of wisdom were closed to him. After repenting, some of the wisdom was again revealed to him. Noah received the wisdom, but afterwards "he drank of the wine and was drunken and uncovered."[111] He then gave wisdom to Abraham. who, by means of it, served the Almighty. But then his son Ishmael provoked the Lord. The same with Isaac, who received the wisdom, but his son Esau also provoked the Lord. As for Jacob, the wisdom was not complete inasmuch as he married two sisters.

He gave wisdom to Moses of whom it is written: "He is trusted in all my house."[112]

The civilization of the Tower of Babel, by virtue of this wisdom, provoked the Lord and built a tower. They did various kinds of mischief until they were scattered over the entire face of the earth and there was no wisdom left.

But in the age of Aquarius, The Force, The Holy One, will cause the Wisdom to be disseminated in the world, and all peoples of the world will make use of the power for useful and worthwhile purposes as it is written: "And I will set my spirit within you,"[113] in contrast with the generations of old, who used it for the ruin and exploitation of the world.[114]

While the Zohar and the verse quoted point to the reappearance of the Wisdom, by what method or teaching will "all peoples of the world" acquire this Wisdom?

Rabbi Jose and Rabbi Judah entered a cavern and at the far end found a book hidden in the cleft of a rock. Rabbi Jose brought it out and caught sight of seventy-two tracings of letters which had been given to Adam. The two began to examine the book. No sooner had they studied only two or three of the letters then they found themselves contemplating that supernal wisdom. But as soon as they began to go into the book more deeply, a fiery flame struck their hands and the book vanished from them.

When they came to Rabbi Shimon they told him what had occurred. Rabbi Shimon replied: The Lord does not desire that so much be revealed to the world, but when the age of Aquarius will be near at hand, even little children will discover the secrets of the wisdom. At that time it will be revealed to all, as it is written,[115] For then I will turn to the peoples a pure language![116]

The Jew shall, in the future, taste from the Tree of Life, the taste of which will come through the Zohar, the Book of Splendor.[117]

Taken all together, the Zohar may prove to be the key as a viable instrument in achieving man's ultimate objective, nothing less than peace and harmony sought through the aching millennia.

So we have rediscovered the Force, the Wisdom. But where are the people who possessed this awesome power? Where did they disappear to? Why can't we find any trace of them? Or did they follow the usual way of all flesh and simply die as most of earth's inhabitants who leave barely a trace of their existence?

Why, we might ask, are we so interested in Atlantis in the first place? After all, we do not seem to be so preoccupied with details of our own grandfathers and their grandfathers before them? The answer, perhaps, is life. Throughout the ages, humankind has speculated about life on other worlds. Unfortunately or otherwise, these other worlds in our own planetary system seem barren. A much broader question, however, is whether there could be planets around other stars elsewhere in the universe.

Throughout history, there has been much speculation on the origin or purpose of the planets. While this question is dealt with more thoroughly in my book on astrology, meanwhile no one knows for sure which if any of the theories presented are correct. What interests us here most, however, is the possibility of the existence of life elsewhere other than life or intelligent forms as we see it on earth. Strangely enough, just when so many scientists are probing for evidence of extraterrestrial intelligence or life forms, a great number are becoming increasingly outspoken about the possibility of its existence. A study of life in the universe, up to now a subject of fiction books, has already begun. It is no longer a question of wondering if there could be somebody out there. The problem is how to establish the first inter-planetary dialogue. The immediate challenge to man is to contact beings on such a planet, inasmuch as our presence has been revealed by our development of radio and television emanations into outer space in the last forty years. Astrophysicists are being encouraged in their probe for life in outer space by new discoveries. The presence of a great number of complicated organic molecules in the universe void earlier theories that such life forms could not exist in space. It might well appear to us that the cosmos contains a great deal of unexpected and unpredictable entities.

However, from a kabbalistic world view of our universe this alone would not signal the existence of other populated worlds. While it would appear to be logical, it is not probable. Intelligent forms to control the universe with the awesome power and wisdom of the Force must be contained within a corporeal, physical body form as we here on earth are. It is precisely the lack of this wisdom that permits a scientist to believe that Earth is a doomed planet. The death of the sun is inevitable they claim, and as it burns itself out, we here on earth face the prospect of freezing to death. Mass migration into outer space is certainly an awful alternative. Acquiring the wisdom is a more reasonable one.

If the existence of other populated worlds is improbable, then where else can we turn in our attempt to locate but a single extraterrestrial signal. Remember we Kabbalists are scientists, not science fiction writers. Even our theories must of necessity not conflict with proven findings if not based on observations and findings. What I can say at this time, is that millions of movie-goers insist on viewing movies which deal with and resemble extraterrestrial life forms and life systems. Who can say that this interest is not the forerunner of things to come?

One of the most remarkable and space-like descriptions of other human life forms I have ever read or heard about appears in the Zohar. This tale and description could very well become the basis for future research.

Similarly the sea is full of different creatures, as it is written:[118]

How manifold are Thy works, O Lord!
In Wisdom hast Thou made them all;
The earth is full of Thy creatures.
Yonder sea, great and wide,
Therein are creeping things innumerable,
Living creatures, both small and great.
There go the ships;
There is Leviathan whom Thou hast formed to sport therein.

Rabbi Nehorai the Elder once went on a sea voyage. The ship was wrecked in a storm and all in it were drowned. He, however, by some miracle, went down to the bottom of the sea and found an inhabited land where he saw strange human beings of diminutive size; they were reciting prayers, but he could not tell what they said. By another miracle he then came up again. He said: "Blessed are the righteous who study the Torah and know the most profound mysteries. Woe to those who dispute with them and do not accept their word." From that day on whenever he came into the house of study and heard the Torah being expounded, he would weep. When they asked him why he wept, he would say, "Because I was skeptical about the words of the Rabbis. I did not believe the existence of seven lands with inhabitants different than ourselves. Now I fear me for the judgment of the other world."[119]

By no means has the Zohar yielded up all its mysteries. Even if we put aside the profound question of sea travel of possibly hundreds of thousands of feet deep into the sea to discover an existing civilization, there remain questions whose answers will surely raise more questions than the answers given.

However, before our investigation should proceed, let us examine the sage and some clues to the inner recesses of this miraculous Rabbi Nehorai, a tannah who lived in the second century and is referred to three times in the Mishnah and in other sections of the Talmud.[120] Most of his statements are aggadic in nature. However, one of his statements commenting on the age of Aquarius is worthy of mention. "In the generation of the age of Aquarius, young men will insult the aged, old men will rise in the presence of the young: daughters will rise against their mothers and daughters-in-law against their mothers-in-law. The face of the generation shall be as the face of a dog, and a son will not be abashed in the presence of his father."[121]

This is a gloomy description for the epitome of human intellectual achievement. If the age of Aquarius points the way to an era of enlightenment as the Zohar seems to indicate, how does one reconcile these two pictures of the same point in time?

He was called Nehorai (light) because he enlightened the eyes of colleagues in knowledge. It was precisely for this reason that he wept when he entered the house of study. He recalled the words of Rabbi Shimon who also wept and said, "Woe unto him who meets with that period (age of Aquarius); praiseworthy is the portion of him who encounters and has the spiritual capacity to be cast with that time."[122] Rabbi Shimon explained this paradoxical remark as follows: Woe unto him who meets with that period, for the revelation of the enormous cosmic light of energy shall be an agonizing torment for those not prepared to deal with it. Praiseworthy, however, are those who shall merit the joy-giving light of the King. Rabbi Shimon confirmed that the Messianic Era will bring with it a Light representing the infusion of spiritual enlightenment through all the worlds. For those ill-prepared to meet the age of Aquarius, the challenge of an age of enlightenment will suffer pain and distress, the likes of which the world had never experienced.

Rabbi Nehorai experienced a close encounter of the real kind. His contact with aliens of an advanced civilization, a society that can survive in an engineered environment moved him to tears. He realized that a civilization of a higher degree of development than presently known to us suffered the fate of all those ill-prepared to handle the profound wisdom. Here were the remnants of the peoples of the Tower of Babel. A living testimonial as to what can happen to an advanced culture when the spiritual ideals of the Force, the eternal Wisdom, are misused.

The destruction of Atlantis as described by Plato was the inevitable result of mistreating and abusing the eternal wisdom, as so many civilizations before them. Adam, the peoples of the Great Deluge and the society of Atlantis, referred to in the Bible as the Tower of Babel civilization and the revelation of this wisdom in the Age of Aquarius caused Rabbi Nehorai to weep. "Woe unto those ill-prepared to deal with it."

The race is now on as to who shall be the first to capture this wisdom and enslave the others. Recalling what had happened in the past, King David wrote: "The Lord is our refuge and strength, a very present help in trouble. Therefore we will not fear, though the earth does change and the mountains be moved into the heart of the seas."[123]

25

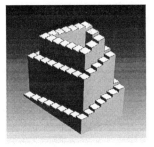

TELEPORTATION

THE NEW AGE OF PHYSICS TELLS US THAT PARTICLES, OR mass as such, do not exist. Rather everything in the universe is energy. Things that we observe are really only mental structures and have form only so long as they are observed as such. Strange as it may sound, this phenomenon is now accepted truth.

We discover that the closer we examine energy, the more easily it disappears into consciousness. The physical world continues to exist. This existence should be viewed as an effect and not a cause of things; as a vessel of energy and not the energy itself.

Taking this concept one step further, energy is an expression of thought and intelligence. Unfortunately, we are not prepared to deal with our physical world in terms of intelligence or thought. It is too great a step at this moment in time to jump from a physical perception of our universe to one which in reality is metaphysical. Seeing things around us as energies or intelligences as opposed to energy fields will require an enormous adjustment. When we relate to the aura of humans which is magnetic, we are truly discovering the internal intelligence and cosmic force of the individual.

Spiritual people or persons with unusual psychic abilities are attuned to this universal source of energy and consciousness. What this really means is that the usual *klippot* (coverings) which surround the average person are not present. Through spiritual activity demonstrated by their "Desire to Share", they have removed these obstructions.

Consequently, these people are oftentimes able to effect and influence serenity, a sense of feeling good, and elevated states of awareness in and around others. The ordinary individual fails to radiate this kind of energy or intelligence, notwithstanding the fact that, as the Talmud remarks,[124] "each person has a physical aura that extends four Amot" (88 inches).

The nature of energy and intelligence and to what extent they coexist as expressions of a singular force will likely disturb many readers of this book. However, there is a growing tendency among researchers to agree that the mind and the brain are not the same. Intelligence as such cannot be found within the framework of the organic brain. The enormous network of neurons and nerve responses in the brain can be mapped, detected and followed by scientists. Intelligence and consciousness itself continues to elude them. The cells, molecules, subatomic particles and other physical segments have very little to say as to what is really going on in the brain. These external entities seem merely to transfer or make manifest the intelligence. Similarly, energy fields serve as channels through which internal intelligence forces find their expression.

This inner intelligence within one's own magnetic field also flows out of the individual's body. This might be compared to a heat wave which travels out of an incandescent metal object. Man's physical body lives within this energy field. The sphere of activity extends as far as seven feet within the immediate environment. This phenomenon is the aura which is, in reality, an image of the energy intelligences of one's life processes. They represent a transcendence from the physical domain of matter. And even though they are bound up with and connected to the structure and content of the body, they have their own metaphysical laws and principles concerning time, space and motion.

From the Kabbalistic world view of intelligence energy, these auras have been known to extend themselves beyond the usual limitation of several feet. In fact, if you're still not certain as to what I have been alluding to, let me state it as subtly as I can, teleportation.

Teleportation is the theoretical transportation of matter through space by converting it into energy and then reconverting it at a terminal point. Can one actually be transported through space? Does one really appear to others at other ends of the earth? Does it not seem to us that the mind or as I prefer to call it, the intelligence factor, is not limited by space in the dream state? The dreamer can apparently travel through space. He can either go forward or back in time. In our dreams we may make contact with people or relatives who have since passed on.

While this out-of-body experience is not quite similar to the phenomenon of teleportation, nevertheless a separation has been brought about. In addition we must admit to the differences between a waking state and sleeping or dreaming state. Recent research indicates that mental telepathy functions far better during the sleeping state than the waking state. Nevertheless, the point being made is that one does experience and find oneself separate from one's physical body. Out-of-body experiences are now being explored in dream laboratories. The two principal research laboratories conducting experiments to determine the accuracy of out-of-body travel are the Maimonides Medical Center in New York and the University of California.

Returning to the phenomenon of teleportation, I can say that for most of us we have gone through this experience at one time or another. How many times have some friends remarked to us that they could have sworn that they saw us at a place where they had been. Yet we are certain that they must have mistaken us for someone else. Undoubtedly, the person they saw, was someone that "probably looked just like you". In some cases the determination of our presence is rather emphatic, but to their dismay, it really wasn't us. Was this an illusion, or was the person really in two places at the same time?

The study of teleportation has not been taken seriously by Western science. The Kabbalah, on the other hand, considers the possibility of energy-intelligence transfer as something very real and cites several illustrations where energy-intelligence of one individual became manifested elsewhere.

> And the two angels came to Sodom at evening; and Lot sat in the gate of Sodom; and Lot saw them, and rose up to meet them.[125]

> Rabbi Isaac put the question, "Why did Lot run after them?" The answer is that Lot saw the image of Abraham and therefore ran towards them.[126]

There is no indication from the Zohar that Lot had hallucinated or suffered some sensory deprivation. On the contrary contends the Zohar, Lot knew all too well that his recognition of strangers and further hospitality could mean his death.

> I have taken note of their behavior towards their fellowman, which causes all men to avoid setting foot in Sodom and Gomorrah; for if anyone were detected offering food or drink to a stranger, the people would cast him into the deepest part of the river.[127]

In fact the Zohar questions Lot's generosity, by asking

> Would not the townspeople have killed him, and meted out to him the same treatment as they did to his daughter? For Lot's daughter once offered a piece of bread to a poor man, and when it was found out, the people of the town covered her body with honey, and left her thus exposed on the top of a roof until she was consumed by wasps.[128]

Obviously Lot was not going to take any chances. But upon seeing his righteous uncle, the Patriarch Abraham, he disregarded any consequences that may have arisen out of his hospitality. Abraham, representing the chariot of Hesed, would have no difficulty in transferring and establishing his intelligence magnetic field in Sodom.

Another example of teleportation provided by the Zohar relates to the purchase of a place for burial by Abraham, the Patriarch, for his wife Sarah.

> So the field of Ephron, which was in Machpelah, which was before Mamre, the field, and the cave which was therein, and all the trees that were in

the field, that were in all the borders round about, were made unto Abraham for a possession in the presence of the children of heth.[129]

Rabbi Judah discoursed on this verse and said: Abraham recognized the cave of Machpelah by a certain sign, and he had long set his mind and heart on it. For he had once entered that cave and seen Adam and Eve concealed there. How did he recognize Adam and Eve inasmuch as he never met them before? (They had died long before). Answered Rabbi Judah: He knew that they were Adam and Eve because he saw the form of Adam very clearly, and while he was gazing at the form, a door opened into the Garden of Eden. He perceived the same form standing there also near the door. Now, Abraham knew that whoever looks at the form of Adam cannot escape death. For when a person is about to pass out of this world he catches sight of Adam and at that moment he dies. Abraham, however, did look at him, saw his form and yet survived. He saw, moreover, a shining light that lit up the cave, and a lamp burning. Abraham then coveted that cave for his burial place, and his mind and heart were set upon it.[130]

If we choose to accept the words of the Zohar, the whole proposition becomes less incredible. If we admit that, at one time or another, we have all felt and undergone a similar experience with a person no longer among the living, or had the *deja vu* sense of feeling "that's happened to me also," acceptance will come easily. Could it not be another hallucination of extrasensory perception? The Zohar, in this lengthy discourse goes to great lengths to remove any doubts as to what Abraham really saw.

From a Zoharic standpoint, Abraham did not hallucinate. He definitely saw Adam and Eve.

What seems to emerge from the foregoing Zohar is that teleportation exists although the energy intelligence has become eternally separated from the corporeal body by death. I guess we might compare this case of teleportation to a live TV program, where the participants are transferred into the home of the viewer without regard to distance. Some years later, although the participants may have died, the forms of them continue to be projected over television waves.

Men of science are well aware that we have not discovered the limits of form transmission as indicated in the Zohar. Therefore, I feel that such a theory applied will survive the many serious research and investigative projects that this book shall initiate.

It would seem to the reader to be stretching the laws of teleportation a bit when he is asked to consider a verbal conversation that could take place between the corporeal living and energy intelligence of a deceased. Yet this very phenomenon is described in the follqwing Zohar:[131]

> And the field and the cave that is therein arose,[132] that is, there was literally an arising before the presence of Abraham. Up until that time nothing had been visible, but now what had been hidden rose up and became visible. Rabbi Shimon said: "When Abraham brought Sarah in there for burial, Adam and Eve arose and refused to receive her. They said: "Is not our shame already great enough before the Lord in the other world on account of our sin, which brought death into the

world, that you should come to shame us further with your good deeds?" Abraham answered: "I am already destined to make atonement before the Lord for you, so you may nevermore be ashamed before Him." Forthwith Abraham after this, buried Sarah his wife to wit after Abraham had taken upon himself this obligation. Adam then returned to his place, but not Eve, until Abraham came and placed her beside Adam who received her for Abraham's sake.

Clearly, in the tale of Machpelah and a good many other cases detailed in the Zohar, there is more at work than extrasensory perception, spirit possession, reincarnation and hallucinations. Can the reader of this book admit that teleportation might well be that something more.

The Kabbalah abounds with intriguing tales of teleportation and the vast knowledge necessary in its implementation. Unfortunately, there have been grave abuses committed in the name of spirituality. Recently there has been an upsurge in the interest to learn about paranormal powers, achieving altered states of consciousness and other paranormal phenomena. These have been all legitimate pursuits, but in their enthusiasm to reach their goals, they have innocently become involved with less desirable movements. In the process they have been misled.

There have been down through the ages highly advanced spiritual teachers like the Ari, Rabbi Ashlag and Rabbi Brandwein. The majority of their students received only a limited degree acceptable to their level of spiritual awareness. Students would have to demonstrate their degree of sharing and understanding of the concept "love thy neighbor". This would be an indication whether they had the ability to correctly make use of the information before it was made available. The followers of these masters would be given certain teachings as they were preparing themselves to use this wisdom wisely.

The sinking of the continent Atlantis mentioned elsewhere in this book, served to illustrate how this wisdom, and the misuse thereof, resulted in the eventual destruction and disappearance of this civilization.

The question likely to be raised at this time is: "Are we to accept the Zohar, writings of the Ari, and other known Kabbalists as accurate?" There cannot be one answer for all. The mystical expression, "when the student is ready, the master will appear" holds truth for all that seek it. For the student ready to accept the Kabbalah, the Kabbalah will reveal itself.

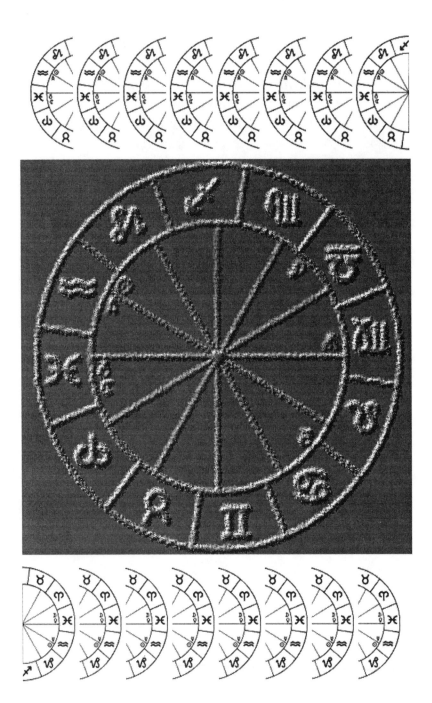

26

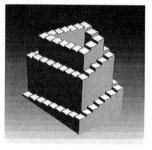

DISCOVERING OUR SOULMATE

FROM THE VERY BEGINNING OF CREATION MORTALS HAVE yearned and searched for their true soulmates. For ages man's love songs have always included a good many melodies whose lyrics speak of soulmates. The songs make the promise that one day soulmates will materialize and bring about a beautiful and lasting relationship. According to some women and men, their real-life experiences verify the idea of one soul divided and once again reunited.

In this chapter we shall explore the origin of soulmates and the methodology for discovering one's soulmate. There is no doubt that one of the most intimate and knotty of human relationships is that of marriage. Immensely rewarding at its best, exceedingly depressing at its worst, marriage offers the extremes of individual happiness and human bondage — with more or lesser degrees of each in between.

Are both extremes predestined for us? Must one person

find the joy of marriage and the other experience the tragedy of this institution? On what, if any, are the circumstances based? When is marriage advisable or inadvisable? Can I tell in advance whether there is anyone else with whom I could be as happy, or happier in marriage than with my intended spouse?

It is probably correct to assume that the majority of marriages are entered into because of an irresistible physical attraction. This explains the high divorce rate in our modern society. A successful marriage must rest upon an understanding of the reincarnation process. One should be well mated not only physically but also spiritually. However, before I provide some clues that can prevent a thoughtless entry into marriage, let us investigate the primal framework of soulmates.

Taken by and large, the soul doctrine expounded by the author of the Zohar provides an enormous fountain of light on the subject of soulmates. The Zohar teaches the pre-existence of all souls since the beginning of creation. Indeed, it goes so far as to assert that the pre-existent souls were already pre-formed in their full individual intelligence while they were still hidden in the womb of eternity.

> When it occurred to the Creator to create the world, all the souls of the righteous were concealed in the divine idea, every one in its peculiar form. When He shaped the world, they were actualized and they stand before him.[133]

Strange as it may seem the concept of extra-terrestrial intelligence was first formulated by the Zohar. The idea that souls are in essence intelligent energy forces has already taken root by virtue of the profound interest displayed by modern scientists. The idea is natural enough. It has certainly occurred to everyone who has contemplated the question of intelligent life in the universe. According to the Zohar these intelligent life forces existed long before creation. In fact, souls are nothing more than varied degrees of the "Desire to Receive" created in the Endless World[134]. Rabbi Ashlag points up to the idea that all life forms are nothing more than aspects of intelligent energy forces. Desire is intelligence.

What took place after these forces became actualized? How did these life intelligences become manifest in our universe? The Zohar provides a precise description of the ultimate physical expression of these metaphysical intelligent beings.

> When the soul is about to descend to this world, it first goes down to the terrestrial Garden of Eden and sees there the glory of the souls of the righteous, and then it goes down to *Gehinnom* [Hell] and sees the wicked who cry "Woe, woe", and find no compassion. That holy form [the internal energy Force], stands by him until he emerges into this world, after which it keeps him company and grows up with him. All initial souls are compounded of male and female. When they go forth into the terrestrial world, the initial soul is divided into two separate entities, the two elements are separated. The intelligent life forces of the male function become clothed in a male corporeality and the female intelligent life force in a female corporeal body. If the man (male) has achieved a level of spiritual consciousness, both male and female intelligent forces will again become united as one harmonious unit. The male has found his soulmate. It is then that he truly meets his mate and there is a perfect union both

in spirit and flesh. But if he is not worthy, she is
given to another, and they bear children whom
they should not.[135]

Herein lies the secret of the soul's yearning for its true
soulmate, whose identity and whereabouts will become known
when the male has achieved a particular level of spirituality or
altered state of consciousness. The male soul desires to be reunited with his female counterpart. For only then does the initial
soul succeed in returning to its original state of wholeness. The
female soul already is endowed with the level of consciousness of
Binah and consequently does not have to strive for a higher level
for this purpose.

This information somehow seems to surface to the conscious mind during that state of spiritual elevation. Rabbi Haim
Vital stated that in one of his intimate discussions with his
teacher, Rabbi Isaac Luria, he was told that "my soul was spiritually superior to that of some of the most exalted supernal angels
and that I could achieve a much higher level of altered states of
consciousness. When questioning the Ari as to my incarnated
soul, he replied "Your soul is that of Don Vidal de Tolosa [second
half of the 14th century Spanish Rabbi and commentator on
Maimonides]. The reason for my reincarnation is to correct
[*tikune*] and amend the disbelief I had in the wisdom of the
Zohar. From the words of the Ari I understood that in my prior
lifetime I had a deep and penetrating mind. During my present
sojourn, I am very lax in making use of my innate ability, that of
deep penetration.

Insofar as my present wife Hanna is concerned,
she is a reincarnation of Rabbi Akiva's father-in
Law, Kalba Savu'a, one of the wealthiest men in
Jerusalem. The latter's opposition to his daughter

Rachel's marriage to Akiva led him to cut them both off. Abandoned to extreme poverty, Rachel once even sold her hair for food. Rachel made her marriage to Akiva conditional upon his devoting himself to Torah study.

The reason for my present wife is that the soul of Rabbi Akiva and mine are of one origin. He is closer to me than all other incarnated souls within me. And because Kalba Savu'a was a homosexual, he returned as a woman. And because her (Hannah's) incarnation is one of a male, there is absolutely no possibility for her to give birth to sons. Regarding to her giving birth to girls, this is also impossible unless another female soul become incarnated within Hannah.

However, continued the Ari, Hannah will die. And when I [Haim Vital] shall achieve the level of Ruah, the same altered state of consciousness of Rabbi Akiva, I shall then merit my soulmate. She will be Rachel, the faithful wife of Rabbi Akiva. And from this marriage shall come forth your faithful son, Shmuel, who shall set down all my writings. You will then merit worthy children.[136]

What seems to emerge from the foregoing is the importance of the male reaching an altered state of consciousness. This in turn provides the setting for children to be born of a higher elevated state of spirituality. The soulmate (female) must be sought out so that patterns of *tikune* may be fruitfully played out. The separation of the sexes, which comes about as souls prepare to enter the terrestrial realm, provides the opportunity whereby each entity might experience the testing of earth's proving grounds. It is the male entity that will learn and ulti-mately earn the right to a reunion with his divine other half. This is the male's true soulmate, your better half if my reader happens to be male.

It is with the faithful soulmate that we shall finally share complete fulfillment. In the reunion of male and female, the ulti-mate circuit of intelligent energy will have come about. And along with it the realization of a fulfillment beyond anything which we may ever know in any experience here on earth.

It is precisely this search and yearning which provides us with an opportunity to learn that love is not emotion or passion alone. In time we begin to understand that love is not self-satis-faction nor initially sex. Within this seeking process we may encounter our soulmates over and over again. Sometimes they appear as parents, as sisters, lovers, children and sometimes even as enemies. The particular relationship in any given reincarnation is a learning experience that hopefully brings about correction and altered states of consciousness. Some will learn real love through many incarnations, while others, more fortunate, may not have to go through human bondage in search for their soul-mate.

Must one person find joy in marriage and another experi-ence tragedy? Are these frameworks of marriage predestined? The answer lies within one's search for spiritual growth. The fulfill-ment and joy of marriage depends completely upon finding one's soulmate. This reunion comes about through experiencing altered states of consciousness. The ultimate circuit of intelligent energy forces has then become firmly established. This then paves the way for the birth of spiritually- minded children, the joy of which is beyond any material pleasure one may ever experience.

Now what happens with the majority of earth-bound persons who have no understanding of the survival of the human spirit, reincarnation? Well for one, the opportunity or possibility of finding one's soulmate, according to the Zohar,[137] is rather nil. So the enjoyment of marriage is elusive. Furthermore the ignorance of the wisdom of the Kabbalah brings with it consequences that I'm certain thinking individuals will make every effort to avoid. After all, most marriages do not appear to be a bed of roses.

Just what does lie in store for those who have not achieved an altered state of consciousness? Throughout this book, I have made an attempt to draw the reader to an understanding of the profound intelligence that is contained both in the sperm and egg of humankind. This intelligent energy force contains the entire metaphysical as well as physical DNA of the individual. What power!

> As we have come so far, we must now disclose the hidden paths of the Lord of the universe, which the children of men know not, though they are all within the way of truth, as it is written: "For the ways of the Lord are upright; the righteous shall walk in them, and the transgressors shall stumble there-in."[138] Those who undergo transmigration and are driven out from the other world [because they refused to propagate themselves] without feminine partners how do they manage to find wives in this world, seeing that no female partner is preordained for them, as for other men? When a man divorces his wife, he causes a defect in the stone of the heavenly altar. As the male who undergoes transmigration and is driven (divorced) from the

other world, so he meets a woman who has suffered a similar fate, driven (divorced) from her
husband. Thus it is possible for the divorcements
to unite themselves one with the other (i.e. the
divorcement of the man's spirit in heaven and of
the woman on earth). Concerning this mystery it
says: "And hath written to her a bill of divorcement and gave it to her and sent her out of his
house, and she departed from his house, and
went and became another man's wife."[139] What
is the signi-ficance of "another"? It points to the
words, "from the region of another (*aher*) that if
he does not strive to spiritually elevate himself,
there will be a development and he will not be
her last husband (he will die).[140]

For the non-spiritual man, a divorce seems to be his lot
and consequence. Does this, then, imply that marrying a divorcee
indicates the human bondage circumstance we mentioned
before? Of course not. Then why does this seem to be the impli-
cation stated in the aforementioned Zohar. The secret revelation
of another passage in the Zohar should allay any fears of one
marrying a divorcee. While at the same time raising other questions, information concerning the mystical realm of reality can
serve as a tool in our search to achieve reunion and the fulfillment of ourselves. The ultimate purpose, both of the married
and the non-married state, is the achievement of altered states of
consciousness. This is probably one of the safest routes to provide
man with the freedom of will and power of choice. One of the
most important aspects of reincarnation is its recognition of free
will. An inaccurate assumption made by many who accept the
tikune and reincarnation principle is that all of life has already
been predetermined. The results of such conclusions are mentally
paralyzing. The restrictions placed upon us in our present life-

time are direct results of mistakes and errors of the past. Through a proper and accurate understanding of the tikune process, the ancient conflict of free will verses predeterminism is resolved. On a birth level of consciousness the radius of free will is largely determined by the *tikune* process of former lifetimes. However, once the individual has escaped the original state of reincarnation and has entered a higher level of spirituality the natal restrictions no longer apply. The intelligence energy force dictating and programming the metaphysical and physical DNA lies on a natal frequency. As such, once the incarnated soul has elevated itself to another level of consciousness, the printout of the natal DNA no longer applies inasmuch as former lifetime actions affect the soul on the level in which the errors and mistakes occurred. If the level of consciousness of a particular soul was in a state of *Nefesh* at birth and in its present lifetime achieves a level of *Ruah* we are actually now relating to another person, another frame of re-ference, Consequently, it becomes crystal clear that in marriage relationships and in everything else, man is completely free to do as he will; what makes the difference is the determination to achieve altered states of consciousness. Once this happens, a new computer printout takes over with a new set of principles. A completely different DNA structure becomes manifest permitting a new set of circumstances that can result in a life of accomplishments and fulfillment .

Let us now return to the Zohar[141] and what it has to say about previously married women.

> Old man, old man! If thou art to reveal mysteries, speak out without fear! ... We have said that the intelligence life form [the internal energy force of the sperm] of a man is left in the woman who was his wife. Well, what becomes of it? Supposing she marries again, is it possible that two different

intelligence life forms of two men should dwell together in one woman? ... Is the force of the first husband entirely lost? Nay this cannot be. The same problem arises even when the widow does not marry again. What becomes of her husband's life form which cleaves to her? All this must now be explained....

When the second husband's intelligence enters into the body of the woman the intelligence of the first husband contends with it, and they cannot dwell in peace together, so that the woman is never altogether happy with the second husband, because the intelligence force of the first one is always pricking her, his memory is always with her, causing her to weep and sigh over him. In fact, his spirit writhes within her like a serpent. And so it goes on for a long time. If the second intelligence prevails over the first one (that means the second union is one of soulmates), then the intelligence of the first husband goes out. But if, as sometimes happens, the first conquers the second, inasmuch as the first union was one of soulmates, it means the death of the second husband. Therefore, we are taught that after a woman has been twice widowed no one should marry her again, for the angel of death has taken possession of her though most people do not know this. Friends, I am aware that on this point you may well object that in that case the second husband's death was not in accordance with fairness by Divine Judgment. It is not so however. It is all decided by fair trial, whether the one spirit should prevail over the other or be at peace with it; but he who marries a widow is like unto one who ventures to brave the ocean during a storm without a rudder or sails, and knows not whether he will cross safely or sink into the depths.

In other words, ignorance of the law, whether physical or metaphysical is no excuse. It is incumbent upon all of us, cautions the Zohar, to understand the laws and principles governing soulmates. The price of ignorance is enormous, sometimes even causing untimely death. This startling revelation concerning the intelligence of the sperm and its unyielding energy force after the death of the first husband is far-reaching. Still more remarkable is the fact that although the internal energy intelligence of the sperm has been severed from its source, the first husband, it continues to play havoc and reign destruction upon subsequent husbands. Only when the first husband was not the soulmate of this woman, can the energy circuit of the second marriage, which is one of a reunited soul mating, overpower and overcome the intelligence energy of the first husband; a miniature star war taking place within the womb of this woman. The extraordinary thing about all this is that the wife herself may never even know why she is "never altogether happy" with the second husband. Her decision to marry again was no doubt the result of much deliberation and soul searching. Nevertheless, she was determined not to remain alone despite her fulfilling life with her first husband. Alone; there is something barren in the word, something that seems to be so very sterile. Remaining alone is perhaps the saddest phrase for one after love. Whatever the *tikune* reasons are for her to remain alone, the second husband should have explored the matter of soulmates more thoroughly. As the spiritual incompatibility becomes more intense, divorce may seem advisable, after considering all other factors involved, namely: level of spirituality, children, consultation with a marriage counsellor. Certainly not because of someone else waiting in the wings is there an indication of soulmate possibilities. Marriage is more serious than most people think. In the instance we just mentioned, death may come prematurely to the second husband if his investigation reveals that there is a strong possibility that his present wife may have already travelled through her present lifetime with her soulmate.

This is precisely the reason the Zohar warns that 'a woman who has been twice widowed no one should marry her again'.

There is the strong possibility that her first husband was her soulmate and his intelligence-presence was felt during the second marriage causing the death of the second husband. However, if the second marriage was terminated by divorce, then we have no real basis by which to assume that the first marriage was indeed a soul marriage.

27

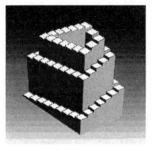

CLUES OF SOULMATE MARRIAGES

WILL MARRIAGE AT THIS TIME BE ADVISABLE? SHOULD I marry the boy or girl courting me? How can I be sure? Questions that married or would-be married persons have asked of themselves.

For whatever reason, the thought had been dropped only to be raised again when it was too late. So what is there to do?

The first obvious step is to begin connecting with the real self. Who am I? For if I haven't the faintest idea what really makes me tick, then how, in heaven's name, can I dream of knowing the other half of myself. If the half of a soulmate is myself, the part that I'm directly connected with, and I haven't got a clue as to who I really am, am I to presume that knowledge of my counterpart is something that I shall hopefully acquire. Wishful thinking.

We have a right to know who and what we are. Furthermore, the Ari[142] considers acquisition of this information for ourselves extremely important for our well-being and happiness. In this way no one can fill our minds with traumatic fears or play upon our lack of confidence in ourselves.

Although many people are of the opinion that they enter life as new human beings, this may not be the case. After all, are we not conditioned by submerged psychological difficulties, fears, suppressed traumas, and a host of idiosyncrasies? Where did it all come from if not from the personal experiences of former lifetimes? It appears to me that all experiences seem to be programmed and part of an overall scheme of which we are only partially aware.

However, if we haven't successfully learned all there is to know about oneself, what advice can the Kabbalah offer by which we can consciously become aware of our soulmate? The decision to become marriage partners has been made. The details of the wedding have reached the planning stage. The date is set and the place of the wedding ceremony has been chosen; the invitations printed and mailed to all the invited guests and relatives. The couple now sit back and enjoy this carefree period which may never again be theirs.

Several days before the wedding date doubts begin to arise. There have been several nasty confrontations. Nothing really important, but serious enough to have second thoughts as to whether this is what I really want. Perish the thought demands the rational psyche of ourselves. The invitations have already been mailed out. You just can't tell all your friends and relatives not to come because you changed your mind. Furthermore, what are you going to do about the wedding reception, which has been so tastefully and lavishly arranged. Can you imagine the embarrassment this will cause for the parents? No! Think no more. All will be well. It's going to work out.

Are these familiar thoughts that went through your head just prior to your wedding date? Is this the kind of thinking that now makes you doubt whether you want to go through the marriage affair at all?

Well, be prepared to be entering matrimony with someone other than your soulmate. Now, I'm not saying there is anything necessarily wrong with not marrying one's soulmate. The Zohar seems to indicate that most marriages take place with someone other than one's soulmate. So infrequent are soulmate marriages that the Zohar goes to great lengths in an attempt to clarify how soulmate marriages come about and the progeny of such matrimony.

> When David committed his great sin in taking Bath-Sheba, he thought that it would leave its mark forever. But the message came to him, "The Lord hath put away thy sin, thou shalt not die;"[143] i.e. the stain has been removed. R. Abba put this question to R. Shimon: 'Since we have been taught that Bath-Sheba was destined for King David from the day of the creation, how come the Lord first gave her to Uriah the Hittite?' R. Shimon replied: Such is the way of the Lord; although a woman is destined for a certain man, He first allows her to be the wife of another man until the time of the soulmate arrives (he has elevated himself spiritually). As soon as that time arrives, he departs from the world (he dies) to make way for the other, although the Lord is loth to remove him from the world to make way for the other man before his time arrives. This is the inner reason why Bath-Sheba was given to Uriah first.[144]

The Zohar's account of this most famous of all Biblical love stories is most interesting inasmuch as it goes far beyond the superficial tale of two lovers. Rabbi Shimon reaches into the inner recesses of the soul's yearning for its true soulmate. He defines marriage as a step by which two individuals unite their forces in the struggle to advance spiritual understanding and help each other discharge their respective *tikune* debts. The Zohar affirms that no major human relationship is the result of chance, but rather is a direct result of a *tikune* process that became established at the time of the creation of the world. A marriage where the participants simply cannot bear to be without each other all of the time is an exemplification of soulmates in its highest degree. It is an episode in a serial begun long before. The need to be together all of the time is made necessary by the *tikune* process. While Bath-Sheba was married to Uriah the Hittite, David, whose soul knew the identity and whereabouts of its soulmate, yearned to be reunited and felt a deep need to be together again. The *tikune* process had governed their separation. Now at last, they would be united again.

However, what was to become of Uriah, her husband, when David reached the level of spirituality necessary to become reunited with Bath-Sheba? "As soon as that time arrives, he departs from the world (he dies) to make way for the other." From passages such as these one can deduce the principle of choice by which a marriage partner should and must make in the *tikune* process of soulmates. Uriah should have known in advance that Bath-Sheba was not his soulmate. Consequently, he should have taken the required step to avoid his untimely death.

Divorce as laid down in the Bible is one of the 613 precepts that provide the individual with tools towards one's *tikune* correction. This is not to say that all males now take this initial step and divorce their wives. What is indicated by the Kabbalah is the necessity for knowing the reincarnation process. And furthermore, just what steps one must take to avoid the pitfalls of an explosive *tikune* situation. The termination of his marriage by divorce would have prevented his untimely death. Within the *tikune* program death for Uriah seemed inevitable. However, Uriah may have had other lessons to learn this time around, possibly more important than the relationship problem at hand. Divorce would have been his answer. He did not choose to make that decision.

The right of self-determination is seen by the Zohar as one of the cardinal tenets of Judaism. Divorce is still considered by many people as sacrilegious. Rabbi Shimon considers the matter of divorce not only as a moral right, but also as one cosmically attuned to the *tikune* process of soulmates. The right of man to demonstrate free-will and self-determination in terminating a marriage is still rejected in many societies. Many a hostile argument has been waged over it in most families where divorce has occurred. The consequences of such a belief are at times devastating and psychologically paralyzing and ultimately spiritually demoralizing.

The more comprehensive world view by the Kabbalah as provided by its reincarnation principles will prepare the individual in his long journey through marriage There need not emerge the kind of bitter struggles that usually accompany the unsettling effects of divorce. At the same time, for true soulmates, the knowledge of the *tikune* process and the reincarnation principle can only strengthen the already existing close ties between the marriage partners. It is information that one can ill-afford to neglect or ignore.

Regarding this matter of David and Bath-Sheba, a further point must be raised. Did David sin in his longing desire for

Bath-Sheba while she was still married to Uriah? What of the commandment, "Thou shalt not covet thy neighbor's wife"?[145] Did not King David himself declare, "Against thee, thee only, have I sinned, and done this evil in thy sight."[146]

It is this new disclosure, at once strange and forbidden, which we encounter as one of the most paradoxical of all areas covered by the Zohar. If, indeed, Bath-Sheba and David were designated soulmates at the time of creation, a marriage truly made in heaven, then how could David have ignored the prohibition against coveting one's neighbor's wife? This point needs to be stressed, for it makes clear the enormous depth of the reincarnation and *tikune* process. The mystical conception of the Torah is fundamental for an understanding of the paradox now facing us. The Zohar, employing every device of that mystical precision with which the Kabbalists read the Bible, infused extraordinary revealing meanings into the words of the Psalms.

> King David said: "Against thee, thee only, have I sinned, and done this evil in thy sight".[147] The significance of this is as follows. It is possible to commit sins which are offenses both against the Lord and man; also one can commit sins which are offenses against man but not against the Lord; but there are also sins which are committed against the Lord only. David's sin was of this last kind. Perhaps, however, you will be inclined to question this, saying, "But what of his sin with Bath-Sheba? Did he not sin against her husband — to whom she was now prohibited — as well as against the Lord?"

> To this query there is an answer, and it is this.

According to tradition, Uriah, as was the custom with the warriors in Israel, gave his wife a bill of divorcement before he went out to battle, and so David did not sin against Uriah in the sense of perfidiously robbing him of his wife. And therefore we read: "And David comforted Bath-Sheba *his wife*"[148] which is proof that she was considered as David's lawful wife, destined for him since the beginning of time.

Thus his sin was an offense against the Lord alone. And in what did that offense consist? Not in that he commanded Joab his General to send Uriah in the forefront of the battle so that he might be killed — for David had a right to do that, as Uriah called Joab "my lord Joab" while in the king's presence, which was disrespectful. The sin of David lies in that he did not have Uriah killed then, when he disgraced King David, but rather let him be killed by the sword of the children of Ammon[149]; for on every Ammonite sword was engraved a crooked snake which was their god. Said the Lord to David: "Thou hast imparted strength to that abomination;" for when the sons of Ammon had killed Uriah and many other Israelites, and the sword of Ammon prevailed, the pagan god had been strengthened by David.[150]

Consequently, Uriah, in granting a divorce immediately may never have been placed in the position where he then insulted King David. In turn, this caused him a death sentence for insulting David.

Another source that may shed light upon our attempt to find indications of soulmates is the writings of the Ari. "When a new soul enters this world, meaning a soul that comes to this world for the first time, his soulmate accompanies him. When the time approaches for them to be joined in matrimony, she will appear without any difficulty. They will instantly fall in love with each other and marry.

However, should the male incur a *tikune* debt, and require a reincarnation, his female soul counterpart will return with him and assist in his *tikune* process. This time around however, he will encounter obstacles all along the way before he meets up again with his soulmate. Inasmuch as he incurred a *tikune* or debt, there are metaphysical cosmic forces that will make every attempt to prevent this soulmate marriage."[151]

These forces have come about by one's negative actions that incur a *tikune* debt. Payment or reaction to negativity is the prevention of a union of soulmates which indicate and influence harmony in the cosmos. By living a negative lifestyle in a prior lifetime he has brought upon himself a cosmic negative influence that makes his reunion with his soulmate all the more difficult. He himself is the cause of his own misfortune that prevents happiness with his soulmate from becoming a lover's reality. When any one or part of our universe departs from its balanced structure so that it endangers the harmony of our cosmology, a pattern of imbalance occurs. More precisely, the *tikune* law of action and reaction applies. Consequently, the balance and harmony that a soul marriage provides for its participants is reduced as a result of the male's inharmonious activities.

And this is what is referred to as a second marriage. It is a second attempt by the male to enter into eternal matrimony. For she is truly his soulmate, second time around.[152]

And now we can understand that when the marriage does take place, and they truly share and expand in all their thoughts and actions, going forth together to accomplish a common goal that will benefit others, this indicates a true and everlasting soulmate. If this was not a soul marriage, harmony and peace could not reign supreme. And when it does, they are truly soulmates. The harmony of the universe is maintained by balance.

28

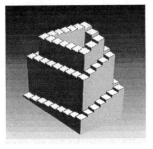

COSMIC SOULMATES

PEOPLE ARE BEGINNING TO REALIZE THAT THERE EXISTS IN our universe an awesome, metaphysical power, sometimes beyond the realm of control. The reader of this book has come to the realization that many of his shortcomings in life or aspects of well-being are directly related to a predetermined *tikune* process. The seeker of enlightenment desires to make use of the many laws and principles of the metaphysical world which are at work in his own personal life.

The question that now arises is how can I find the key which will say who could marry whom to realize a marriage filled with joy that knows no boundaries? Astrology, or the science of cosmic influences affects all areas of human experience, and more precisely the province of matrimony. It can have much to say, for example, about the relationship which will soon begin to develop between two people contemplating marriage. Statements like a Leo should not marry a Cancerian is sheer nonsense. Kabbalistic astrology could not nor would it say who could marry whom.

What we can say is that there are certain areas of our predetermined *tikune* in which the parties are going to find living together a strain. There will be other areas of life in which they may
be particularly well-suited. If nothing else, astrology will point up
some enlightening factors which make up one's personality stim-
ulating the two parties to take a hard look at his and her true
feelings before bringing the affair to the point of marriage.

The charts reveal much about the interrelationship
between them. Hopefully, lovers will find this information as a
valuable short cut, revealing some characteristics of each other's
personalities which might otherwise take years to emerge. This
book will advise, in a general way, about a timely cosmic month
or day for the marriage. From a kabbalistic world view of our
universe, the cosmic influence prevailing on the day or evening of
marriage will strongly affect the entire lifetime of this union.
Again, this information is not intended as a rigid guideline as to
what one should or should not do. This knowledge can only
attempt to clarify the situation for the individuals. The participants ultimately must make their own decisions.

An important issue that must be explored before we can
fathom the inner cosmic influences of our cosmos is: "Why are
the planets of the solar system, the sun and the moon, the only
bodies considered as viable intelligent energy sources when deli-
berating soulmates for marriage? The Zohar[153] broadens our perception of cosmic entities so that we begin to think of them in
terms of intelligence instead of just energy in the form of cosmic
rays which are essentially streams of particles.

In the Kabbalistic view[154] humankind like all other life
forms are part of an inseparable whole. The intelligence of celestial bodies implies that the whole too, like human beings, are
intelligent. Man is seen as the manifested proof of cosmic intelli-

gence. Inasmuch as there are seven varied forms of intelligence in our universe, these seven heavenly bodies[155] (Sun, Moon, Saturn, Jupiter, Mars, Venus and Mercury) are the designated Celestial channels by which the seven cosmic intelligent forces become manifest on earth.

Therefore, a birth chart is a map of the heavens as the new-born child would see it at the moment of its birth. As just stated, man and the celestial bodies are part of an inseparable whole. When a particular planet rules at the time of birth, the cosmic influence of the planet provides us with an interface of our own essential essence. The internal intelligence prevailing at the time of birth provides us with a comprehensive picture as to who we basically are.

It therefore becomes apparent that the seeker of true soul-mates must be given, along with the access to this information, the means to use it and the spiritual understanding necessary to guarantee a soulmate marriage. The mystery of the technique alone, however, does not necessarily insure the perfect marriage. An elevated altered state of consciousness along with a spiritual awareness must, of necessity, be achieved before the male can become worthy of his soulmate.

From the days of Abraham, the Patriarch, some 3800 years ago, there was virtually no change in astrological theory. The planets, as in ancient times, remain the principal life-forms of our universe. Their movements are used to explore and elaborate upon the present. From a Kabbalistic-astrological world view of our universe, each moving planet was given a special relation-ship with a fixed sign of the Zodiac. The sun and the moon rule one sign each, and the other planets rule two signs each.

From a Kabbalistic point of view there is no controversy

among Kabbalists over the discovery or influence of the three evidences of their direct cosmic presence.

The field of astrology and Kabbalah both point to a unity between man and the universe. This is not the place to examine in detail the contributions of the Kabbalah in this field, for its collected works represent a lifetime of study alone. My attempt in this chapter is to draw attention to the *Sefer Yetzirah* and its commentators concerned with the universal cosmic principles as the underlying and motivating intelligence energy force for a successful and happy marriage. On the basis of these fundamentals, a record of the channels along which cosmic energy intelligences are transmitted from the outer world to the inner nature of man is provided. It indicates how the two partners will react to experience as it clashes all around them, how they will react with each other. All of us, as if by an uncontrollable instinct know that the final and sum total of our happiness lies in the mystery of ourself. The root or inner source of human conduct is always hidden from the eye. There is no real way of scientifically proving anything about the internal nature of man. The human soul, its objectives, its motives and characteristics, continue to avoid any form of detection.

Consequently, when so eminent a scholar and author of the geonic period, Saadiah Gaon authored a commentary on the *Sefer Yetzirah* providing us with an in-depth penetration of the cosmos, one can feel that herein lies the key to the mystery of cosmic energy intelligence. Saadiah Gaon's real importance lies in his being the first medieval rabbi to make any attempt to reconcile the Torah with reason and human happiness.

> This is the rule concerning the four elements. Fire and earth detest each other; fire and air love each other; fire and water simply hate each other; earth

and water endear each other; earth and air abhor each other and fire and fire feel happy with each other.

Aries (*Taleh*), Leo (*Aryeh*) and Sagittarius (*Keshet*) are masculine fire signs.

Gemini (*Teumim*), Libra (*Moznaim*) and Aquarius (*D'li)* are masculine air signs.

Cancer (*Sartan*), Scorpio (*Akrav*) and Pisces (*Dagim*) are female water signs.

Taurus (*Shor*), Virgo (*Betulah*) and Capricorn (*G'di)* are female earth signs;"[156]

The sun has always been the most powerful of all the celestial bodies . It portrays the personality so vividly that an amazingly accurate picture can be given of the individual who was born when it was exercising its cosmic influence through a known, and according to Saadiah Gaon, predictable channel of a particular sign of the Zodiac.

Furthermore, states Saadiah,[157] "although one Hebrew letter created Aries and the Hebrew month of Nissan, Aries does not necessarily rule throughout the Hebrew month of Nissan. The sign of Aries makes its influence felt in the cosmos beginning with the spring season and continues for just a trifle over 30 days. Then Taurus and Gemini follow for a similar period of 30 days respectively, completing a total of 91 days, seven and a half hours. The summer season begins with Cancer, followed by Leo and Virgo for a similar period. So it is for Libra, Scorpio and Sagittarius starting with the fall season. Finally, Capricorn, Aquarius and Pisces for the winter season. This, of course, does not mean that the sun sign alone is to be taken into account. The

Hebrew months based on a lunar-Solar system also exert their cosmic influence. This particular matter is more fully described in my book on astrology.

However, studying your sun sign for a glimpse of your soulmate is what we are considering here. Only a natal chart calculated for the exact hour and minute of your birth can provide the complete detail of your personal chart. The sun is not the only element in analyzing human behavior, but it is surely the most important single factor.

Briefly stated, just what is a sun sign? A particular region of the Zodiac — Aries, Gemini, Aquarius, etc. — in which the sun was located at the moment we drew our first breath.

Taken all together, who matches up with whom? Well, for one, the fire signs feel very happy with each other as does earth and water, and fire and air. This compatibility is quite understandable. Life forces here on earth testify to its harmony.

Earth requires water in its endeavor to fulfill its objectives in providing sustenance for the world. Air must fan a fire for the fire's continued existence. One intelligence force complementing the activities of the other. The lack of either intelligence force determines and brings about a lack and incompleteness in the other. One needs and requires the other. There is no ego involved. Both elements recognize the inadequacy of themselves. This is a true soulmate.

However, in marriage when one of the partners seems to manage it alone, we know that soulmates are not involved. If mutual interest in spiritual or other matters that pertain to the welfare of others does not exist between them, a soul marriage is out of the question.

However, at this point it is important that I make mention of the reincarnation principle concerning marriages outside the framework of soulmates. The female half of any soulmate is not required to return to assist her male counterpart. Females are not required to be reincarnated. "The cleansing of the soul in purgatory is sufficient for females", states the Ari.[158] In the case where the male must be reincarnated to fulfill the *tikune* process, the female counterpart of this soul may elect to remain where all souls, having no further debt to pay, remain. So for those of you, not married to your soulmate, don't be disappointed. Your present time around fits into the overall program of the *tikune* process.

To return to our subject of cosmic clues to soulmates, the ground rules as laid down by Saadiah Gaon are exceptionally clear. Persons with an Arian influence are enthusiastic, generous, and have an instant smile. At the same time, the Arian is conscious only of himself. They may be quick-tempered — they are no diplomats — and will at their worst be completely absorbed with themselves. Their needs come first. An Arian may be so intent on looking after himself that he could forget to consider his closest friends.

Superficially speaking, these are accurate descriptions of a strong Arian character. Nevertheless, the contradictions are equally visible. If the true Arian is so generous, then how do we include the trait of selfishness among his internal basket of characteristics? The answer to this and many other obvious contradictions concerning *all* the sun signs are more fully described in my book on astrology. What we are concerned with here is not so much the "why" of things. The purpose of this chapter is to provide the reader with enough material and information to determine if indeed their marriage or intended matrimony involves soulmates.

Consequently, the knowledge furnished by Saadiah Gaon is intended to provide a cosmic, internal printout for people concerned with the matter of soulmates.

The water signs, according to Saadiah do not interact with Leo, Aries or Sagittarius. Water and fire don't go well together. In fact, according to the Zohar,[159] the internal intelligence of water, which is positive by nature, is intent upon extinguishing all forms of internal intelligence ruled by fire. Fire is negative in essence. Correspondingly, the internal intelligence of fire is determined to prevail over water, sear and dry it up.

Observable water and fire are merely the physical manifestations and expressions of the internal intelligences we referred to. Once the materialization disappears the internal energy intelligence is no longer a viable force. Without its vessel water, the internal intelligence of positivity returns to its potential state of inactivity. In the absence of the physical expression of the flame, its negative internal intelligence reverts to its original motionless state.[160] There is no disappearance of any form of internal intelligence forces. The vessel or the element that permits and makes possible the physical expression of these extraterrestrial (non-physical) intelligences have disappeared. If the water no longer exists, then its internal energy force (intelligence) can no longer express itself. It lies dormant until such time when the physical vessel or channel is again permitted to surface.

This is the essence of continuous conflicts between, say, a Leonine and a Scorpion. Their internal intelligences conflict with each other. Consequently, one or the other must ultimately yield their channel or else all hell will break loose. Therefore, in the final analysis, while they may each learn to live with each other, they seldom if ever complement or fire the enthusiasm of their mate. This is not the definition of a soulmate. There is nothing really complicated or difficult about Leo. He is king and make no mistakes about it. I know! I'm Leo. Leos need the opportunity to express their natural and enormous potential. The water signs simply do not meet the task of fanning the fires.

However, were the Cancerian, Scorpion and Piscean teamed up with the earth signs, each partner would have a better chance of expressing their individual internal intelligence energies. Water was created for the express purpose of assisting mother earth in her flourishing endeavor to provide sustenance to the world.

The land provides the internal intelligence of water, the element of sharing, with the opportunity of expressing itself. One force complementing the other. This could be indicative of true soulmates.

But try uniting a Libran with a Taurean and what do you find. The internal intelligence of a Libran is the character of central column.[161] As such they demonstrate the ability to mediate between others and restore harmony. They are always in the middle, moving from one opposing side to the other. Restless if you may. In their attempt to balance the scales, there is always that long road of the balancing process itself. First one side is higher, then the other. Up and down is this laboring procedure until there is perfect balance. Movement. Never-ending restlessness.

A Taurean embraces and envelops the intelligence of earth. The fabric of this intelligence is its desire to be the recipient of things that go on all around it. It loves to be part of the landscape, a permanent fixture abhorring movement. The epitome of the Desire to Receive.[162] Put the two together and you have the makings of a windstorm. The Taurean will not be rushed or moved as the Libran partner would have it. The intelligence of possessiveness, rather than reaching out, is the decisive energy factor which determines the character of a Taurean. The Libran will have no part of this. Life with a Taurean is too dull and bo-ring. Permit the Libran to fan the fire of a Leo and see them shine and smile.

It's for this very reason that fire signs are not real soul-mates of earthborn intelligent forces. The Leonine is magnanimous; expansive and even interfering. The Taureans would rather be taking care of their immediate needs. The bull seldom rushes forward to take the initiative. He simply wants to be left alone. His internal intelligent force is like mother earth or maybe like the rock of Gibraltar, solid, steady and immovable. So persevering, they will not budge an inch. A Taurean simply could not dance to the same tune as the Leonine.

If you think the Aquarian could face any better with the Taurean, then you have another guess coming. If there is anyone that can really unnerve the Taurean it's the Aquarian. While friendly, they often prefer to remain detached. They are extremely faithful and loyal, but horribly unpredictable. Personal independence is of great importance to them, even to the point of temporarily rejecting intimate and close friends and relatives. People born under this air sign can really toss up a tempestuous wind with their fellow Taureans.

So there you are, soulmate seekers. Saadiah Gaon seems to have provided us with some additional information in choosing our lifetime partner. This is by no means a suggestion on my part, that for those not fitting the description hurry off to the nearest divorce agency. If anything short of divorce, make a serious attempt to understand the positive and negative traits in your relationship. They may be there for the sole purpose of growing spiritually.

BIOGRAPHICAL NOTES

AARON BEN JOSEPH HA-KOHEN SARGADO — also known as Halaf ibu Sargado, Gaon and dean of the Pumbedita Yeshiva, c. 940-60. His antagonist Saadiah Gaon was a great concern of his, and while he was very eloquent and erudite, Saadiah was a much greater scholar, and this Aaron envied. He wrote an Arabic commentary on the Pentateuch, in the same style as that of his rival Saadiah. Maimonides mentions Aaron as one who opposed the view of the Greek philosophers that the universe is eternal.

AARON OF BAGHDAD — (c. mid-ninth century), Babylonian scholar, lived in southern Italy. He is described by Rabbi Eleazar as "father of all the secrets". As to the nature of these secrets, it is clear from *Megillot Ahimo'az*, that Jewish scholars were studying early mystical works before the arrival of Aaron.

ABBA, RABBI — (circa 130 C.E.) Student of Rabbi Shimon bar Yohai who, according to the Zohar (III, p.287b) actually put into writing the words of the Zohar as they were revealed by Rabbi Shimon bar Yohai.

ABBAYE — (circa 270-339 C.E.). One of the most prominent Amoraim; together with his opponent Rava mentioned most often in discourses in the Babylonian Talmud.

ABI-HASIRA — family of Kabbalists, most of whom lived in Morocco. Samuel (c. 1500) lived in Syria. He was known as a scholar of Talmud and practical Kabbalah. Jacob ben Masoud was a Kabbalist, widely known for his piety, wrote *Ginzei-haMelekh* on Kabbalah.

ABARBANEL, RABBI DON ISAAC — (b. Lisbon 1437, d. Venice 1509). Rediscovered the wondrous world of the mystical realm in general and the Kabbalah in particular. Served the Spanish royal house before the expulsion of the Jews from Spain. He succeeded in piercing the iron curtain concealing the mysterious enigmas of redemption cloaked in the *Book of Daniel*. He offered encouragement to Jews following their expulsion from Spain by composing several works concerned with the central desire of that period, the coming of the Messiah.

ABRAHAM, PATRIARCH — (1900 B.C.E.) considered to be the chariot of the Sefirah Hesed (Kindness), as exemplified in the *Book of Genesis*.

ABRAHAM BAR HIYYA — (c. 1130) Spanish astronomer, main astronomical work was *Hokhmat haHizayon*, consisting of two parts. The first part, "Form of the Earth and Figure of the Celestial Spheres" is a review of the seven lands and seven climates mentioned in the Zohar. The second part, "Calculation of the Courses of the Stars", based undoubtedly on the *Sefer Yetzirah*. There is an incident about a clash with his distinguished contemporary in Barcelona, Judah b. Barzillai al-Bargeloni. This occurred during a wedding which Abraham insisted on postponing because the stars were not propitious.

ABRAHAM BEN ISAAC OF GRANADA — Spanish Kabbalist, author of *Brit Menuhah*, the Covenant of Rest, the book's purpose was to provide a systematic basis for the so called Practical Kabbalah. His work was highly regarded by Moses Cordovero and Isaac Luria.

ABRAHAM BEN MOSES BEN MAIMON — (1186-1237) Son of Maimonides, scholar and subsequent leader of the Egyptian Jewish community following the death of his father. After the great controversy erupted in Provence and Spain over the writings of his father, he came to his father's defense. While Maimonides directed all his efforts to codifying the Talmud, his son's view of Judaism was of a mystical nature.

ABULAFIA, TODROS BEN JOSEPH HA-LEVI — (c. 1220-1298) Spanish rabbi and Kabbalist. Abulafia was instructed in Kabbalah by Moses ben

Solomon ben Shimon, and to whom he dedicated his *Gates of Secrets*, a commentary on Psalms. In the opinion of Isaac Albalag, Abulafia was one of the three foremost Kabbalists of his generation. Isaac ibn Latif who lived in Toledo dedicated his famous work *Zeror haMor*, a Bundle of Myrrh, to him. His son Joseph, joined the Kabbalistic circle in Toledo, became friendly with Moses de Leon and was one of the first to receive a copy of the Zohar.

AKIVA, RABBI BEN JOSEPH — (c. 15-135 C.E.) Younger contemporary of Rabbi Gamliel; teacher of Rabbi Shimon bar Yohai, the author of the Zohar *Book of Splendor*; began the study of the Torah at the age of forty, motivated by his wife Rachel, the daughter of the wealthy Kalba Savua by whom he was employed as a shepherd (*Tractate Ketubot*, P. 62b). One of the most prominent leaders (Tanna), his disciples in his academy at Bene Berak numbered some twenty-four thousand (*Tractate Sanhedrin* 32A); he compiled and systemized the topics of Torah Bal Peh (Talmud) known as the Mishnah of Rabbi Akiva (Mishnah, *Tractate Sanhedrin* 3). This work laid the foundation for the final compilation of the Mishna by Rabbi Yehudah haNasi (the Prince). Main supporter of Bar Kochba whom he considered to be the Messiah, in the latter's insurrection against Rome; captured by the Romans and put to death for studying Torah, expiring with the Shema upon his lips. "With the passing of Rabbi Akiva, the crown of the Torah ceased to exist" (*Tractate Sotah* 92).

ALASKAR, MOSES BEN ISAAC — (1466-1542) Talmudist and Kabbalistic poet born in Spain, he fled Spain in 1492 when the Jews were expelled. Alaskar later settled in Egypt, and in 1522 became dayyan in Cairo. That Alaskar knew Kabbalah is apparent from his Kabbalistic explanations cited by Samuel Uceda in his *Midrash Shemu'el* and in several of his liturgical poems. Famous for his book *Hassagot*.

ALDABI, MEIR BEN ISA — (c. 1300) Kabbalist born in Toledo, was the grandson of Asher ben Jehiel. Close ties with Bahya ben Joseph ibn Paquda and Nahmanides. Settled in Jerusalem where he completed his famous work, *Paths of Faith*.

ALGAZI, YOM TOV BEN ISRAEL JACOB — (1727-1802), Kabbalist and Halakhist. Close friend of H.D.D. Azulai, studied under Rabbi Jonah Navon and Rabbi Shalom Sharabi. Algazi was a member of the Ahavat Shalom group of Kabbalists.

ALKABETZ, RABBI SHLOMO HALEVI — (b. 1505 Salonica, d. 1576

Safed), Kabbalist and mystical poet, author of *L'cha Dodi* recited Friday evening, founder of the famous Kabbalistic centre at Salonica. He was a contemporary of Rabbi Joseph Caro, author of the *Shulan Arukh* and the Ari, Rabbi Isaac Luria.

AMARILLO, AARON BEN SOLOMON — (1700-1772) Kabbalist, born in Salonica. Famous for his responsa *Penei Aharon.*

ANGEL, MEIR BEN ABRAHAM — (c. 1560) Rabbi and Kabbalist, born in Sofia and emigrated to Safed where he studied under Hayim Vital.

ANTIBY, ABRAHAM BEN ISAAC — (1765-1858) Syrian Talmudist and Kabbalist, he was born in Aleppo, studied under his father, Isaac Berakhah and Isaiah Daban. In his writings on the Kabbalah, he speculated on the date of redemption. He is the author of Yoshev Ohalim. His works are an important source for the religious life of the Jews of Syria.

ASHER BEN DAVID — c. 1229) Kabbalist, grandson of Abraham ben David of Posquieres, Asher lived in Provence and was one of the most important pupils of his uncle, Isaac the Blind. His most important works appeared under the title *Sefer Ha-Yihud.* They include a lengthy explanation of the Tetragrammaton, *Perush Shem ha Meforash*, an explanation of cosmogony, *Perush Ma'aseh Bereshit.* His works are among the earliest detailed accounts of Kabbalistic ideas. In this respect Asher stands close to Azriel of Gerona. His writings indicate that the Zohar, later revealed by the famous Spanish Kabbalist Moses de Leon in 1290, was already known by the famous Kabbalists.

ASHER BEN JEHIEL — (c. 1250-1327) Acknowledged leader of German Jewry, left Germany and accepted position of Rabbi in Toledo, where he was welcomed with great honor by Solomon ben Abraham Aderet. His piety which is expressed in his celebrated work, *Hanhagot haRosh*, which indicated his heretofore Kabbalistic understanding of the Talmud.

ASHKENAZI, BEZALEL — (c. 1520-1591) Born in Jerusalem, moved to Egypt in 1540 and founded an important school of learning. Among its scholars was the great Lion of Safed, Isaac Luria. Left Egypt in 1587 to become Chief Rabbi in Israel to succeed Hayim Vital. When the famous Rabbi of Egypt, David ben Solomon ibn Abi Zimra went to Israel (c. 1550), Ashkenazi succeeded him as head of the Egyptian rabbis. His most famous and classic work is *Asefat Zekenim.*

ASHLAG, RABBI YEHUDAH — (1886-1955) Famed Kabbalist known as the pioneer of modern Kabbalism, developed a new approach to the understanding of the Lurianic system. His profound yet accessible writings provided the necessary keys in comprehending the Zohar. His translation of the entire Zohar, known as the *Sulam*, facilitated the widespread interest of this sublime and obstruse text. He opened the portals to spiritual Judaism through his sixteen volume textbook called *The Study of the Ten Luminous Emanations*."

AZULAI, RABBI ABRAHAM BEN MORDECHAI — (1570-1643) famous Kabbalist born in Fez from a family of Kabbalists of Castilian origin, wrote three treatises on the Zohar; *Or Levanah* (Light of the Moon), *Or ha-Chamah* (Light of the Sun), and *Or-ha-Ganuz* (the Hidden Light), based primarily on the Lurianic system. Underscored the permission granted for all to enter the gates of the world of mysticism.

BARZILLAI, JUDAH BEN AL-BARGELONI — 12th century Spanish Kabbalist and Halachist known for his commentary on the *Sefer Yetzirah* called *Perush Sefer Yetzirah*. His other works include *Sefer haItim*, which deals with the Jewish festivals which are referred to extensively by later commentaries.

BOTAREL, MOSES BEN ISAAC — 15th century Spanish Kabbalist, whose main work is a commentary on the *Sefer Yetzirah*. This invaluable work stemmed from his desire to enhance the status of Kabbalism.

BRANDWEIN, RABBI YEHUDAH ZVI - (1904-1969) Kabbalist and significant student of Rabbi Ashlag. His vast knowledge of the Lurianic system enabled him to codify and edit the entire writings of the Ari, Rabbi Isaac Luria. Continued with the similar style of translation and commentary of Rabbi Ashlag known as *Maalot haSulam* (Extension of the Ladder) on those works of Rabbi Shimon bar Yohai, which Rabbi Ashlag didn't complete during his lifetime, namely *Hashmotot haZohar* (Various other Writings) and *Tikune Zohar* (Addendum to the *Zohar*). First Jewish settler within the Old City of Jerusalem after the Six Day War.

CORDOVERO, RABBI MOSES — (1522-1570) Also known by the abbreviation REMAK, famed Kabbalist of Safed's "golden age", brother-in-law of Rabbi Shlomo Alkabetz, and one-time teacher of the Ari, Rabbi Luria. His large main work *Or Yakar*, (Precious Light), on the entire *Zohar* has only recently begun to see the light of day. Originator of one of the two basic systems of understanding the *Zohar*. His other major work *Pardes Remmonim* (Orchard of Pomegranates) is a systematic compendium of Kabbalistic concepts surrounding the internal action of the original unified energy force emanating from the Creator. Rabbi Hayim Vital, student of Rabbi Isaac Luria had a dream in which the REMAK revealed to him, that in the age of the Messiah the Lurianic system would prevail.

DAVID BEN ABRAHAM MAIMUNI — (1222-1300) Magid of Egyptian Jewry and grandson of Maimonides. His commentary on the first portion of *Genesis* quotes also from the *Zohar*, indicating the existence of the Zoharic writings before revealed by De Leon.

DAVID BEN ABRAHAM HA-LAVAN — (c. 1300) Spanish Kabbalist, wrote *Masoret ha-berit*, a Kabbalistic work on Reincarnation.

DAVID BEN JUDAH HAHASID — (c. 1340) Spanish Kabbalist and grandson of Nahmanides. Wrote many books on Kabbalah, which he believed evolved from the Castilian Kabbalists. Authored the *Sefer haGevul*, on the *Idra Rabba*, *Or Zaru'a*, a lengthy Kabbalistic commentary on the order of prayers.

DONOLO, SHABBATAI — (c. 913-982) Famed Italian Kabbalist and physician who was born in Oria, Italy. His most famous work on Kabbalah is his book *Sefer Hakhmoni*, a commentary on the *Sefer Yetzirah*. His *Sefer haMirkahot* (Book of Remedies) drew material from his knowledge of *haKarot haPartzuf* (physiognomies) and astrology, which undoubtedly was based on his comprehension of the Kabbalah. His *Sefer Hakhmoni* provides a massive collection of information regarding the study of astronomy; without it, the study of astrology would remain incomprehensible.

ERGAS, JOSEPH BEN EMANUEL — (1685-1730) Rabbi, Kabbalist, who was of Marrano descent, was born in Leghorn, descending from a noble Spanish family. Benjamin ha-Kohen Vitale of Reggio taught him Kabbalah. His Kabbalistic works include: *Shomer Emunim*, *Mevo Petahim* selections from Lurianic Kabbalah and *Minhot Yosef*, rules for the study of Kabbalah.

GALANTE, MOSES BEN MORDECHAI — (c. 1550) Safed Kabbalist, a disciple of Joseph Caro and Moses Cordovero. His main work was *Mafte'ah haZohar*, an index of biblical passages in the *Zohar*. Brother of Abraham ben Mordechai Galante.

GERONDI, JACOB BEN SHESHET — (c. 1340) Kabbalist in Gerona, Catalunia. His most famous work, *Meshiv Devarim Nekhohim*, was referred to in works of Bahya ben Asher and Menahem Recanati.

HAYYAT, JUDAH BEN JACOB — (c. 1450) Kabbalist, he was born in Spain and studied Kabbalah under Samuel ibn Shraga. After the Spanish expulsion he lived in Mantua, Italy. His work, *Ma'arekhet haElohut*, is a detailed Kabbalistic text, which agrees in principle with the views of Menahem Recanati concerning the essence of the Sfirot.

HAYIM ABRAHAM RAPHAEL BEN ASHER — (c. 1720) Sephardi Chief Rabbi and Kabbalist. He published the *Sha'arei Kedusha* of Hayim Vital.

HAYIM BEN ABRAHAM HAKOHEN — (c. 1580) Kabbalist born in Aleppo, his ancestors came to Aleppo after the expulsion from Spain. He was a student of Hayim Vital during his last years in Damascus. He was one of the Rabbis of Aleppo. Wrote numerous works on Kabbalah which include his *Mekor Hayim*, a detailed Kabbalistic commentary on the rules of the Shulhan Arukh.

HAYIM BEN JOSEPH VITAL — (1542-1620) Kabbalist and the only student of the Ari, Rabbi Isaac Luria, born in Safed. His father Joseph Vital Calabrese came from Calabria, South Italy. He studied under Moses Alshekh, his teacher in exoteric studies. In 1564 he began his studies in Kabbalah, at first according to the system of Moses Cordovero. After the arrival of the Ari, Rabbi Isaac Luria in Safed, Vital became his only student, studying with the Ari until the Ari's death on the 5th of Av, 1572. He then began to arrange the Ari's teachings in written form. Vital moved to Jerusalem, where he served as Rabbi from 1577 to 1585. He returned to Safed in 1586 and stayed there until 1592. He then moved to Damascus and remained there until his death. By this time he had recorded all the teaching of his teacher. The writings were assembled into two works. The first was the *Tree of Life* and the second was organized into eight sections called *Sha'arim* or gates. There was the *Mevo haSha'arim*, entrance to the gates and then the eight gates: "Gate one", *Sha'ar haHakdamot*, gate of introduction which includes the doctrine of emanation and creation of the world: "Gate" two and three, *Sha'ar Ma'amarei Rashbi veRazal*, commentaries on the writings of the RASHBI, acronym of Rabbi Shimon Bar Yohai, author of the Zohar and three, on talmudic tractates according to the Lurianic system: "Gate" four, *Sha'ar haPesukim*, commentaries on all parts of the Bible: "Gate" five, *Sha'ar haMitzvot*, commentaries on all the precepts of the Bible arranged according to the order of the Torah: "Gate" six, *Sha'ar haKavannot*, provides the meditation for all prayers and precepts plus the reasons for the precepts in the first place: "Gate" seven, *Sha'ar Ruah haKodesh*, deals with the method and system of mind power, by which things of our universe and all that it contains can be manipulated and brought under control, unification of the Cosmos, utilization of cosmic energy, the *tikune* process and the principles of physiognomy: "Gate" eight, *Sha'ar haGilgulim*, covers the doctrine concerning the soul and its transmigrations, which is what this book is all about. Vital was one of the most important influences on the development and dissemination of later Kabbalah, assuming the position as principle formulator of the Lurianic system.

IBN EZRA, ABRAHAM — (1089-1165) Born in Tudela, Spain, biblical commentator, physician and astronomer. His enormous writings stand as a significant contribution for mankind. Believing in astrology, he attempted to reconcile the belief in cosmic decrees with the concept of free will.

ISAAC BEN JACOB HAKOHEN — (c. 1260) Spanish Kabbalist related to Shem Tov ben Abraham ibn Gaon. Authored books on the evolutionary process and other important Kabbalistic material. Travelled extensively through Spain and Provence collecting the knowledge of Kabbalah from elder Kabbalists, then recording it in many of his writings. It appears that the Spanish Kabbalists were fully aware of the existence of the *Zohar*, authored by Rabbi Shimon bar Yohai, long before it was made public by the sainted Kabbalist Moses ben Shem Tov de Leon in Guadalajara in 1280.

ISAAC BEN SAMUEL OF ACRE — (c. 1270) Kabbalist, Isaac left Acre for Spain where he met numerous Kabbalists and quotes many of their writings. Of significance is his meeting with Moses de Leon concerning the authorship of the *Zohar* by Rabbi Shimon bar Yohai. His major work, *Me'irat Einayim* is a commentary on Nahmanides' mysticism, who, by Kabbalistic tradition, brought the *Zohar*, Book of Splendor from Israel to Spain. Another of his works is *Ozar Hayim*, a mystical diary of visions and revelations. Most of his revelations came while he was in a trance, and many other mystical visions were revealed through his dreams.

ISAAC THE BLIND — (c. 1160) a Kabbalist and son of Abraham ben David of Posquieres, the RABAD. Bahya ben Asher called him the father of Spanish Kabbalah. Shem Tov ben Abraham ibn Gaon mentions that he could sense whether a person would live or die, and whether his soul was among the new souls that have come down to earth or had already experienced transmigrations. (Recanati, *Perush leTorah, VaYeshev* and *KiTetze*). Recanati also claimed that Isaac had received the "revelation of Elijah".

ISCANDARI, ABRAHAM BEN ELEAZAR — (c. 1550) one of the four sons of Eleazar ben Abraham Iscandari (Scandari) who was court physician of Sinan

Pasha, the Turkish governor of Egypt. He maintained a yeshiva in his own home and possessed many manuscripts. Engaged in the study of Kabbalah and copied the *Sifra deTzenuta* of the *Zohar* with a commentary of the Ari, Rabbi Isaac Luria, adding his own glosses.

JOSEPH BEN SHALOM ASHKENAZI — (c. 1300) Spanish Kabbalist, descendant of Judah ben Samuel haHasid, authored a commentary on the *Sefer Yetzirah* and regarded the *Zohar* as a fountain for Kabbalistic material. The Ari, Rabbi Isaac Luria regarded his Kabbalistic knowledge and specifically his conclusion that there must be one cause for all causes.

JOSEPH HAYIM BEN ELIJAH AL-HAKAM — (1830-1909) Baghdad Rabbi and Kabbalist. Wrote some 60 works on all aspects of Torah. Best known for his *Ben Ish Hai.*

KADOORIE, SASSON — (1885-1971) Baghdad Rabbi, was Chief Rabbi from 1927-1929.

KASSIN, RABBI JACOB — Rabbi and Kabbalist, who at a very young age advocated the study of Kabbalah. Chief Rabbi and Haham of the Syrian community in Brooklyn, New York.

LANIADO, RABBI SAMUEL BEN ABRAHAM — (c. 1540) Syrian Rabbi, biblical commentator, known for his works *Ba'al haKelim.* He was a grandson of Samuel Laniado who settled in Adrianople after the expulsion from Spain. He was born in Aleppo, where he became head of the community after the death of the famous Kabbalist, Rabbi Samuel ben Joseph haKohen. His son, Abraham was also a dayyan in Aleppo.

MENAHEM AZARIAH OF FANO — (c. 1609) famous Italian Kabbalist whose work *Ma'amar haNefesh* follows the mystical idea developed by Rabbi Isaac Luria concerning the soul, in that each letter of the Torah represents the upper root of the soul of each individual in Israel. Consequently, each individual soul has its own framework of reference in understanding the Torah.

MOSES, RABBI BEN SOLOMON OF BURGOS — (c. 1230) Spanish Kabbalist and student of the famous Kabbalists, Isaac and Jacob ben Jacob haKohen, and a leading Kabbalist in Castile. His pupils included Isaac ben Solomon ibn Sahula and Todros Abulafia. He thus expressed the relationship of philosophy to Kabbalah: "The level attained by their (philosophers) heads reach only the position of our feet;" His works include a commentary on *Song of Songs*, on the 42-lettered Divine Name and the Mystery of the 13 Divine Attributes.

NAHMANIDES — (Rabbi Moses ben Nahman: abbreviated RAMBAN) — born in Gerona 1195, d. 1270 Akko. Famed Spanish Kabbalist, Talmudic scholar and biblical exegete who adopted a mystical position in the battle which raged around philosophy during the thirteenth century. His commentary on the *Sefer Yetzirah* provides an in-depth comprehension to this abstruse and difficult work on the Kabbalah. His commentary on the Bible cannot be understood apart from a comprehension of the Kabbalah. His opposition to Aristotelianism, which had endangered the very foundations of Judaism in Spain, was completely based on the principal doctrines of the *Zohar*, which legend relates was already known to Nahmanides. The mysteries of the Kabbalah which initially took hold during the latter half of the twelfth century in Provence and subsequently came to full bloom there and in Northern Spain in the thirteenth century was the Creator's beneficence for a reawakening and rebirth of a new life under its influence. Nahmanides played no small role in this new development if not possibly the harbinger of this movement which climaxed a period in the history of the Jews on which they have always looked back with pride when referring to this "Golden Age in Spain".

NEHEMIA BEN HAKANHAH, RABBI — (c. 70-130 c.e.) A student of Rabbi Johanan ben Zakkai (*Baba Batra* 10a). A famed mystic and author of the *Ana beKoah* a recitation included in the morning prayer. This profound mystical prayer is connected with and related to the Seven Sefirot inasmuch as each of the seven sentences relate to a particular Sefirah. This prayer is also included in the counting of the Omer with its significance being the mystical relationship to each day of the forty-nine days that commence with the second day of Passover and end the day before Shavuot. Since the cosmological influence during this period is considered to be totally negative and destructive, the Ari, Rabbi Isaac Luria, explains in his *Book of Meditation*, the use of this prayer in altering the Cosmic influence of these forty-nine days. He has also been considered the author of the famed Kabbalistic text, the *Sefer Bahir*.

PINTO, JOSIAH BEN JOSEPH — (1565-1648) Kabbalist born in Damascus and was for the major part of his life Rabbi in Damascus. He followed closely the system of the Ari as set down by Hayim Vital. His son, Shmuel Vital was his pupil and subsequently married his daughter. He is best known for his work called *Me'or Einayim*.

RABAD — (c. 1125-1198) Rabbi Abraham ben David of Posquieres, known by his acronym RABAD, Kabbalistic and Talmudic authority who lived in Provence. A distinguished authoritative scholar known for his in-depth criticism of Maimonides, produced numerous literary works, *Torat haBayit* and *Baal haNefesh* to mention a few. His commentary on the *Sefer Yetzirah* is of special significance, inasmuch as this work established the RABAD as one of the most prominent figures in Kabbalistic literature. This work (and his probing into the metaphysical strata of Kabbalah) exerted considerable influence on subsequent Spanish Kabbalists. He defined heretofore abstract concepts with a maximum of clarity. For this he attained for himself a special place in history as one of the greatest commentators on the Kabbalah.

RASHI — (1040-1105) Rabbi Shelomoh Yitzhaki. French Torah and Talmud scholar whose commentaries form an essential part of Jewish learning. His writings include *Siddur Rashi, Sefer haPardes, Sefer haOrah, Likutei haPardes* and *Sefer Issur-Vehetter.*

RECANATI, RABBI MENAHEM BEN BENYAMIN — (c. 1350-1440) Italian Kabbalist, whose family originally came from Spain. His main Kabbalistic work was *Perush ol haTorah* (commentary on the Torah), and *Ta'amai haMitzvot* (Explanation of the precepts). He is quoted extensively throughout the writings of the Ari, Rabbi Isaac Luria. The Ari, mentioning *Sefer haRecanati*, tells of an incident where a person, who, on the night of Hoshana Rabba — which according to the *Zohar*, is the time when we can know if our sins have been purified and we shall live for another year - went out at midnight according to the teachings of the Ari. Upon seeing that his full shadow didn't appear and the head was missing, he knew this was a sign that he needed to attain a higher degree of purity. He returned to the house of study and wept and repented wholeheartedly and when he felt cleaner inside he went outside again and observed that his prayers had been accepted as he saw his full shadow by the light of the moon (*Gate of Meditation*, p.307b).

SAADIAH BEN JOSEPH GAON — (882-942) Greatest scholar of the gaonic period and important leader of Babylonian Jewry. Saadiah was born in Egypt. After leaving Egypt, he spent time in Eretz Israel and Aleppo from where he proceeded to Baghdad. His Halakhic works are still largely in manuscript form, thousands of scattered parts. He wrote an Arabic commentary on the *Sefer Yetzirah* which was subsequently translated into Hebrew by Moses ben Joseph of Lucena. His work *Emunot veDe'ot* presents his thoughts on the concept of knowledge; he maintains that revelation is necessary. His translation of the Bible is of particular importance, since it is written as a popular translation in order to make it accessible to the ordinary reader. He was also a great innovator in the sphere of *piyyutim* (hymns).

SARUG, ISRAEL — (c. 1550) Egyptian Kabbalist, knew the Ari, Rabbi Isaac Luria while the latter was in Egypt. From the writings of Hayim Vital, he began to formulate his basis of the Lurianic system. He founded a whole school of Kabbalists, among them the most famous Kabbalists of that time, such as Menahem Azariah Fano, Isaac Fano and Aaron Berechia ben Moses of Madena. He claimed he could recognize the transmigration of the people he met. Wrote a commentary on portions of the *Zohar*.

TAYYIB, ISAAC BEN BEYARNIN — (c. 1760) Rabbi, Kabbalist, from Tunis. Authored a Kabbalistic work and commentary on Avot and the Passover Haggadah.

TOLEDANO, HAYIM BEN HABIB HAHASID — (c. 1600) originating in Toledo, Spain, Rabbi and Kabbalist, copied and disseminated the Kabbalistic work, *Yerah Yakar* of Rabbi Abraham Galante.

UCEDA, SAMUEL BEN ISAAC — (c. 1530) Talmudist and Kabbalist, born in Safed, studied Kabbalah principally with Hayim Vital and Elisha Gallico. He established a yeshivah in Safed where Kabbalah and Talmud were studied. He also spent time in Aleppo. Among his works are *Midrash Shemu'el* on AVOT, where he quotes some of the early Spanish scholars.

UZIEL, RABBI JUDAH — (c. 1620) son of Rabbi Joseph, Rabbi, Kabbalist and Dayyan in Fez, became Chief Rabbi of Fez.

VALLE, MOSES DAVID BEN SAMUEL — (1696-1777) Italian physician and Kabbalist, born in Padua, he was considered to have had spiritual powers and received mystical revelations. He is mentioned in documents relating to the Kabbalistic circle of Moses Hayim Luzzatto. Part of his work appears at the end of Luzzatto's *Megillot Setarim*.

VIDAS, ELIJAH BEN MOSES DE — (c. 1540) Kabbalist and one of Safed's greatest. He was a disciple and friend of Moses Cordovero, who he referred to as my teacher. His *Reshit Hokhmah*, is one of the outstanding works on morals in Judaism. He wrote extensively on the *Zohar*.

VITAL, JOSEPH — (c. 1500) A talented scribe, was especially noted for his maintaining the highest standards of *Kavanot* when writing tefillin, which was widely known as *Tefillin Rav Calabrash* (Tefillin of the Rabbi of Calabria from where his family stemmed). His tefillin were highly praised by the Ari, Rabbi Isaac Luria, who claimed that most of the Jewish world at that time received their spiritual nourishment and energy from his tefillin. His tefillin were also highly praised by Menahem Azariah de Fano. He was the father of the famous Kabbbalist Hayim Vital. The Ari once told aim Vital that he would have a son who would be an incarnation of his father, Joseph. Therefore it was Shmuel Vital, Hayim's son who actually prepared the writings of the Ari, inasmuch as it was actually his grandfather Joseph who was doing the writing.

VITAL, MOSES BEN JOSEPH — (c. 1590) younger brother of Hayim Vital, Rabbi and Kabbalist in Safed, who assumed a more important role in the Kabbalistic community of Safed.

VITAL, MOSES BEN SHMUEL BEN HAYIM — (c. 1650) Rabbi and Kabbalist who moved from Safed to Egypt, son of the legendary Shmuel Vital, editor of the writings of the Ari. He was known to be a brilliant Kabbalist. However, there are no works that have been left behind.

VITAL, SHMUEL BEN HAYIM — (c. 1600) famous Kabbalist, son of Hayim Vital, distinguished pupil of the Ari, grew up in Damascus where he studied under his celebrated father. He edited his father's writings of the Ari and added many of his own annotations which began *Amar Shmuel* (Shmuel said). Many Kabbalists came to Damascus to study his writings. Around 1665 he went to Cairo where he served as Rabbi. He was in close contact with the wealthy Raphael Joseph Chelebi. A protocol on his exorcism of an evil spirit (dibbuk) in Egypt was published at the end of "Gate" eight, *Sha'ar haGilgulim* of the Ari.

YITZHAKI, ABRAHAM DAVID — (1661-1729) Kabbalist, born in Jerusalem. A grandson of the famous Kabbalist, Abraham ben Mordechai Azulai. He studied with Moses ben Jonathan Galante and Joseph Bialer, grandfather of Hayim Joseph David Azulai, the HIDA. He was Chief Rabbi of Jerusalem, Rishon-le-Zion in 1708 and held the position until his death. He was the author of the responsa *Zera Avraham*.

ZACUTO, MOSES BEN MORDECHAI — (c. 1620) Kabbalist, who was born into a Portuguese Marrano family in Amsterdam. He edited the Zohar Hadash in 1658. He enjoyed great authority as head of the contemporary

Italian Kabbalists and corresponded with Kabbalists in many places. He added many annotations under the name KOL HAREMEZ from his initials.

ZAYYAH, JOSEPH BEN ABRAHAM IBN — (c. 1500) Rabbi and Kabbalist, born in Jerusalem, he completed his *Even haShoshan* in 1538. He then went to Damascus to serve as Rabbi, where he completed two other works; *Zeror haHayim* and *Sha'arit Yosef.*

ZEMAH, JACOB BEN HAYIM — (c. 1580) Kabbalist and physician, he was a member of a Converso family in Northern Portugal. He then went to Safed where he learned Kabbalah. Around 1628 he left for Damascus, studying the Lurianic system under Shmuel Vital. When settling in Jerusalem, he became one of the leading Kabbalists. His works include, *Zohar haRaki'a,* a commentary on the Zohar's *Sifra diZenuta* and the *Idra, Lehem min haSha'mayim,* a compilation of Lurianic customs, *Zemah Zaddik* and *Kol baRamah.*

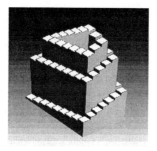

GLOSSARY

ADAM — The sfirot represented as a man, e.g. Keter as the brain, Hokhmah the eyes, Binah the ears, Z'eir Anpin the nose, Malkhut as the mouth.

ADAM AND EVE — From the Kabbalistic point of view, from one undifferentiated soul, after the fall they became two parts of one soul. Soulmates. Adam representing the male principle of drawing energy for sharing; Eve representing the female principle of receiving and revealing.

ADAR — The twelfth month of the Jewish calendar lunar year, sixth from the Jewish New Year, approximating to February-March. Its Zodiac sign is Pisces.

AGE OF AQUARIUS — The Age of Messiah, ushered in by the writings of the Ari Z"L forty years after the expulsion from Spain. From then on many of the limitations and prohibitions surrounding Kabbalistic study were completely removed.

AGGADAH — Name of those sections of Talmud and Midrash containing homiletic expositions of the Bible.

ALEPH BETH — The metaphysical DNA of all creation which channels Light into our world; the 22 letters manifest in the Hebrew writing system.

ALL-EMBRACING UNIFIED WHOLE — The Lord.

ANGELS — Manifested supernal energy-intelligences, beings of Light dedicated to specific purposes who are not subject to Free Will.

ASTRAL TRAVEL — The non-corporeal mode of traveling great distances which transcends time, space and motion.

BAR/BAT MITZVAH — the time at which the aspect of imparting in the soul awakens, age thirteen in the male and twelve in the female.

BE'RICH SHEMAI — A prayer in Aramaic said before taking out the Torah. The power of the prayer is the transcending of time, space and motion, a "time-tunnel".

BERAKHAH — benediction or blessing, the metaphysical connection to the internal intelligent energy of things.

BET DIN — rabbinical court of law.

BODY ENERGY-INTELLIGENCE — The energy-intelligence of the Desire to Receive for the Self Alone.

ASHKENAZI — German, or West, East or Central European Jew, as contrasted with Sefardim. (See also, "PARDES").

BOOK OF DANIEL — The Prophet Daniel lived in Persia at the time of Nebuchadnezor. The book of Daniel contains coded knowledge referring to the Age of Aquarius and the letters of the Hebrew Aleph Beth; the wisdom of the Book of Daniel is sealed until the end of days.

BOOK OF ESTHER — The Megillah of Esther, the festival scroll of Purim telling the story of the salvation of the Jews of Persia. It speaks in length about the giving of gifts and charity; it unveils many great secrets and contains coded information on overcoming all evil.

BOOK OF SPLENDOR — (Zohar) Of the Zohar it is written: In your compendium, Rabbi Shimon Bar Yohai, The Zohar, the Book of Splendor, shall Israel and the world in the future taste from the Tree of Life, which is the Book of Splendor. And the world shall go forth from its exile with mercy (Zohar III, 124b).

BOTZ — World of "botz" (mud). This physical mundane plane which maintains its grip as our daily reality.

BRAIN — The physical corporeal vessel which permits the manifestation of the mind.

BREAD OF SHAME — The shame felt when receiving something for nothing. The whole purpose of coming into this world is to remove the Bread of Shame.

CABLES — various means for the transference of positive metaphysical energies to man (such as, prayer, meditation, Shabbat, the Festivals, etc.).

CANCER — Sign of the zodiac corresponding to the Hebrew month of Tammuz in which the dreaded disease of the same name may begin due to vulnerability caused by a crack in the security shield of positivity. A time in which extra care must be taken to avoid falling into arguments and other negative activities.

CAUSE — That which brings about the revelation of a level.

CENTRAL COLUMN — synthesizer and synthesis of the left and right (negative and positive energies). The connecting link between the right and left, positive and negative, male and female.

CHARIOTS — Entities that embody both metaphysical and physical levels of energy-intelligence.

CIRCULAR CONCEPT — The balance between left and right, negative and positive, brought about by use of restriction. Central column.

COLUMNS — (Right, Left and Central) Macrocosmic pipes or lines of energy corresponding to positive, negative and balancing energies, similar to the proton, electron and neutron in the microcosmic atom.

CONSCIOUSNESS — Levels of awareness. As the soul sheds the veils of negativity caused by the Desire to Receive for the Self Alone, higher levels of understanding and awareness are made manifest.

ALTERED STATE OF — A state of conscious awareness that transcends the five physical senses. An enhanced and elevated level of consciousness brought about by developing the Desire to Receive for the Sake of Sharing and complete circuitry and connection to the Light.

BODY — The Desire to Receive for the Self Alone.

COSMIC — The highest state of awareness in which the universe is conceived of as one all-embracing unity, in which all souls are recognized as one indivisible, interrelated and interdependent whole beyond the confines of time, space and motion. Quantum consciousness, where past, present and future are unified in the present.

SOUL — The Desire to Receive for the Sake of Sharing.

CORRECTION — The task of bringing cosmic and individual harmony to the universe in a state of perfection.

COSMIC DANGER ZONES — Cyclically occurring zones of time, which manifest strong negative influences and which can be overcome or, at least mitigated, by the knowledge of Kabbalah and the use of Restriction.

COSMIC INFLUENCES — Just as the moon influences the tides of all bodies of water on earth on a physical level, and emotional states on a more subtle level, so do the myriad cosmic influences combine and interweave, metaphysically as well as physically, to shape the destiny of humanity and the universe. Man, with the proper knowledge of Kabbalistic tools, has the ability to take control over these and make manifest a higher parallel reality of harmony and peace.

CREATOR — the source of all positive energy to the total exclusion of any negative energy.

DA'AT — Knowledge.

DALETH — "Poor", the fourth letter of the Hebrew Alphabet, symbolizing the earth with the connection of either the Shekhinah or Z'eir Anpin.

DAVID, KING — Second King of Israel and Judah, suceeding Saul. Author of many Psalms. King David's son by Bat Sheva, King Solomon, constructed the First Temple. Chariot of Malkhut.

DELUGE — The great flood described in the Biblical account of Noah, Genesis 7.

DESIRE TO RECEIVE FOR ONESELF ALONE — negativity. The aspect of drawing or taking. In our universe all is made up of the "Desire to Receive". On the physical level, a "desire to receive for itself alone", characterized by selfishness, egotism, materialism in man must be transmuted to a "desire to receive in order to impart" — a balance and harmony between receiving and imparting permitting the individual to draw into himself the positive light of the Creator.

DESIRE TO RECEIVE FOR THE SAKE OF SHARING — (Desire to Impart — positivity) The aspect of giving, characteristic of the Creator, as opposed to the Desire to Receive for the Self Alone.

DNA — Deoxyribonucleic acid. Bound in double helical chains forming the basic material in the chromosomes of the cell nucleus, it contains the genetic code and transmits the hereditary pattern.

DOR DE'AH — The "Generation of Knowledge", the Generation of the Flood which as a group reincarnated at the time of the Tower of Babel, again during the Exodus, and now during the Age of Aquarius.

DVEKUT — "Cleaving". Fulfillment of circular concept whereby union is brought about between the Light of G-d and man.

EGO — The individual as self-aware, self-centered. From the kabbalistic point of view, ego is the manifestation of the Desire to Receive for the Self Alone. Ego is the underlying factor for the limited expression of our five percent consciousness. Our ego convinces us that all our decisions and activities are the direct result of our conscious mind and thought.

EMPTY SPACE — vacuum, non-revealment of the Lightforce. This "gap" represents the energy-intelligence of vulnerability.

ENCIRCLING LIGHT CONSCIOUSNESS — Superconscious encircling light takes off where inner light consciousness ends. The all-pervading consciousness of the cosmos — where information of past, present and future meet as one unified whole — extends beyond the inner light consciousness of humankind. It is precisely encircling light consciousness that we find most in our lives.

ENDLESS, THE — The Infinite All-Embracing Unity.

ENERGY TRANSFER SYSTEM — The following energy transfer systems within the esoteric systems as prescribed within the esoteric wisdom of the Kabbalah created and written on special parchment by qualified scribes, to provide cosmic consciousness and pure awareness to those seeking a higher level of cosmic intelligence through power of Tefillin, Mezuzoth, Megilloth and Sefer Torah.

EVIL EYE — There are some men specially fitted for the transmission of blessings, as for instance a person of a "good eye". There are others who are specially fitted for the transmission of negativity and curses. "On whatever their eyes fall their curses are confirmed.... Hence ... a man should turn aside a hundred times in order to avoid a man with an evil eye...." The priest was able to recognize such a man because he had one eye slightly larger than the other, shaggy eyebrows, bluish eyes and a crooked glance and was known by the name ET.

FIVE SENSES — The senses of our body consciousness: sight, hearing, smell, taste, touch.

FORCE, THE — Lord, the Light; the All-Embracing Unity.

FRAGMENTATION — Disunity and disruption brought about by the divisive and destructive manifestation of the Desire to Receive for Oneself Alone.

FREE WILL — The ability to choose between manifesting the Desire to Receive for Sharing or the Desire to Receive for Oneself Alone.

G'MAR HA TIKUNE — the final redemption of Israel, the ultimate peace and harmony in the world. (See Correction)

GOLDEN CALF — A calf of gold worshiped by the Erev Rav while Moses was at Mount Sinai.

GVURAH — The sfirah of Judgment power, might. The second of the seven sefirot. Left Column, Chariot of Isaac.

HEISENBERG'S UNCERTAINTY PRINCIPLE — In quantum mechanics, the principle that it is impossible to measure simultaneously and exactly two related quantities, as both the position and momentum of an electron. From a Kabbalistic point of view, the basis of this dilemma is a fundamental rule. The conclusion brought to the forefront is the notion that things can be everywhere at once; no space, as the Zohar determined.

HESED — Mercy, Loving-Kindness. First of the seven sfirot. The right column Abraham, the Patriarch, is Hesed's chariot.

HEI — The second and fourth letters of the sacred Tetragrammaton, the first Hey representing the sfirah Binah and the second, the sfirah Malkhut.

HOD — Splendor. Fifth of the seven sfirot, the left column. Aaron, the High Priest is Hod's chariot.

HOKHMAH — Wisdom. The second sfirah following Keter and is the architectural bottled-up energy of total creation.

IQ — (Intelligence Quotient) — IQ testing was designed in the 1920's principally for children and young people. They are not very useful or successful in testing adults. The reason for their limited success with children is the limited scope of exposure to life that most children experience. While intelligence tests are tremendously useful, and will doubtless be with us for a long time, nevertheless, mental health experts are still not sure what these yardsticks actually measure.

INTELLIGENCE — Reflection on the ways of cause and effect in order to clarify the final result.

JERUSALEM — Holy inasmuch as it portrays a constant flow of internal energy. The energy center of the world.

KABBALAH — The inner soul of the Torah. From the Hebrew l'kbl, meaning "to receive".

KABBALISTIC MEDITATION — Special techniques of meditation which are fully described in the Writings of the Ari Z"l.

KAVANNAH — The need to center one's inner world with the attention appropriate to the situation or connection.

KETER — Crown. The link between the Lightforce and the brain is Keter, the seed of all physical manifestation and activity.

KLIPPOT — (Sing.= klippah) Shells, evil husks created by man's negative deeds which cover and limit man in his spiritual development. The barriers between man and the Light of the Force.

LEFT COLUMN — the column (channel) through which are drawn all metaphysical energies. (See Desire to Receive).

LIGHT BARRIER — The Desire to Receive for Oneself Alone which impedes the revealment of the Light.

LIGHT — The source and force of all energy, mental and physical with an intrinsic characteristic of sharing.

LIGHTFORCE — See Light.

LURIANIC KABBALAH — The system of Kabbalistic inquiry and practice as established by Rabbi Isaac Luria. Emphasizes the more active side of prayer. It deals basically with the sparks of Light which elevate in prayer. It is found in Kabbalistic literature that prayer is like an arrow shot upward by the reciter with the bow of kavannah.

MALKHUT — Kingdom—the tenth and final sfirah from Keter. The sefira in which the greatest desire to receive is manifest and in which all correction takes place. The physical world.

NESHAMAH — Third of the five levels of the soul. Correlated with the sfirah of Binah.

NETZAH — Victory. Fourth of the seven sfirot. Synonymous with the right column. Moses, symbolized as its chariot.

NON-CORPOREAL BEINGS — Thought conscious extraterrestrial entities without the physical limitations of time, space and motion.

OR EN SOF — The Light of the Infinite (Endless) from which sprang all future emanations. The primal Light in which the souls of man were in perfect harmony with the Creator. A complete balance between the endless imparting of the Creator and the endless receiving of his creations—the souls of man. That of which nothing can be understood and which yet must be postulated.

PARALLEL UNIVERSES — The realm of the Tree of Life reality and the Tree of Knowledge illusionary reality as outlined in Genesis.

PARDES — Biblical interpretation giving the literal, allegorical, homiletical, and esoteric meaning of verses or words of the Bible. The word "pardes" consists of four Hebrew letters: P, R, D, S — the "P" for the literal; the "R" for the allegorical; the "D" for the homiletical; the "S" for the esoteric or Kabbalah. The Hebrew word "Sephard" (Jews generally considered as originating from Spain) is one of the most misinterpreted and misunderstood words ever to have emerged within Judaism. The word "Sepharad" has no original connection with the Hebrew word for Spain. On the contrary, the Hebrew word for Spain, "and the word "Sepharadi" have their origin in the Bible, long before the emergence of the country Spain (Obadia, ch. 1: 20).

The Zohar says: "Four persons entered the Pardes (orchard) concerning the nature and process of creation. These were: Ben Azzai, Ben Zoma, Aher (another, the surname given to Elisha Ben Abuyah) and Rabbi Akiba. Ben Azzai, Ben Zoma and Aher entered the domains of "P"shat, "R"emez and "D"rush interpretations of the Torah. Only Rabbi Akiba entered the domain of "S"od, and he alone survived, but the others who entered PeReD, the world of separation did not survive. It is through the addition of the "S" (Kabbalah) that the word "PeReD" (separation) — is changed to the world of unity, becoming "SepheRad". So one studying the Kabbalah is termed "Sepharadi"; all other Jews belong to the category of "PeReD". Consequently, because of the *tikune* process, one may be incarnated as an Ashkenazi, but if his studies also include the Sod (Kabbalah), then he is in essence a Sephardic Jew. Contrarily, one incarnated as a Sepharadi and neglects or is even opposed to the study of Kabbalah, is considered an Ashkenazi Jew. (Zohar I, p. 26b, 27a).

PLACEBO EFFECT — The effect of a placebo, a harmless, unmedicated preparation, given to a patient merely to humor him, or used as a control in testing the efficacy of another medicated substance can demonstrate the power of the human mind in healing under the given positive suggestion. The placebo effect demonstrates the psychosomatic quality of disease.

QUANTUM —-In the Kabbalistic sense of the word: The meditation techniques of Kabbalah will both permit and induce all of humanity to realize that whatever serves the collective consciousness of humanity also serves the needs of the individual. The substance of "Quantum" is "Love Thy Neighbor." When this is achieved by mankind, the entire universe, both the seen and the unseen, will be revealed as it actually is, a single unified whole. Our universe is perceived as fragmented only because mankind is fragmented.

RA'AYA MEHEMNA — The Faithful Shepherd, referring to Moses.

RADIOACTIVE WASTE — Hazardous materials resulting from man's tampering with the intrinsic balance of the universe.

RASHBI — Rabbi Shimon bar Yhoai.

REINCARNATION — The movement and stages the soul journeys to achieve its *Tikune* (correction).

REM — Rapid eye movements. During sleep, periods of rapid eye movements indicate the occcurrence of dreams.

RESTRICTION — The Central Column energy-intelligence force that establishes and maintains balance in the universe.

ROBOTIC CONSCIOUSNESS — When celestial influences govern the daily activities of man without intervention of his/her intrinsic ability to exercise free will.

RIGHT COLUMN — Hesed. Column that draws the energy of imparting the positive force.

RUAH — Second lower level of soul consciousness. Prior to the sin of Adam which was the negation of the Lightforce, the entire universe existed and remained connected at the level of Ruah, unfettered by the claims of space and time, unshadowed by entropy and death. Correlated with the sfirah of Z'eir Anpin.

SATAN — The personification of the Desire to Receive for Oneself Alone.

SCAN — The method used by the electronic device called a "scanner" which identifies merchandise bar codes by traversing a surface rapidly and point by point with a beam of light thereby examining, identifying and interpreting printed characters and visual images. From a Kabbalistic point of view, the human eye is the window of the soul and as such is a powerful tool for the transmission and reception of the Light channelled by the letters and words of the Zohar. The connection is established at the metaphysical level of our being and radiates into our physical plane of existence. Hebrew reads right to left.

SECURITY SHIELD — When the Shield of David is activiated a protective film of the Lightforce surrounds the individual thereby preventing the invasion of the Dark Lord and its devastating fleet of misery and illness.

SEFER YETZIRAH — The Book of Formation. First known Kabbalistic work containing in concise, highly esoteric language, the entire teachings of Kabbalah. The first written work of the Kabbalah. Attributed to the patriarch Abraham.

SFIRAH (Sfirot, pl.) — A Kabbalistic term denoting the ten spheres or metaphysical channels or vessels through which the Light of the Creator, the Intelligent Energy Force, emanates and manifests itself, and is emanated to man.

SEPHARADI — (pl.= Sepharadim), see PARDES.

SHEKHINAH — the cosmic realm to which an individual may connect and acquire cosmic consciousness, manifested in the dimension of Malkhut.

SITRAI TORAH — (Sitrei Torah) The deepest hidden teachings of the Torah received only through divine revelation.

SLEEP — Permits the soul to temporarily extricate itself from the limitations and uncertainties of the physical body consciousness.

SOUL — The Light clothed in the Vessel of Intelligence.

SPACE-TIME — Where time is now addressed as a gap or empty space.

SPEED OF LIGHT — 186,000 miles per second. From the Kabbalistic point of view, however, light does not travel but is ever present albeit in a state of concealment awaiting revealment. The Kabbalist, therefore, speaks of the "speed" of the revealment of light.

TA'AMEI TORAH — (Ta'amai Torah) The reasons of Torah. The teaching through which one reaches the true inner meanings of Torah and thereby elevates oneself to the highest degrees of spirituality.

TALMUD — The written form of the oral law. The main work of Judaic studies. A compilation of Mishna, Tosfot, Gemarrah.

TAMMUZ — fourth month of the Jewish calendar lunar year, tenth from the Jewish New Year, approximating to June-July. Its Zodiac sign is Cancer.

TEMPLE — A physical structure over the energy centre of the universe acting as the receptacle or receiving station for the Lightforce.

TETRAGRAMMATON — The sacred name composed of the four Hebrew letters, Yod, He, Vav and Hey.

THE BOOK OF FORMATION — See Sefer Yetzirah.

THE POWER OF ONE — The All-Embracing Unified Whole, the Lightforce.

THOUGHT CONSCIOUSNESS — The only true reality which must be considered in a frame of energy-intelligence.

TIKUNE — - The process of correction made by the soul.

TOWER OF BABEL — See Genesis 11:4.

TREE OF LIFE — The point from which the life energy force remains as an all embracing unified whole without the trappings of chaos and uncertainty.

TREE OF KNOWLEDGE — "Good and Evil" phase of our illusionary reality. Here randomness, uncertainty, chaos, rot, disorder, illness and misfortune make their presence felt.

TSHUVA — No individual can ever achieve a completed phase of Tshuva, (a Back to the Future Concept) where the individual comes into total control of his fate and destiny, unless he becomes knowledgeable of the unconscious root psychological processes of the soul along with the knowledge of former lifetimes.

TZIMTZUM — The original Restriction.

UNCONSCIOUS PROCESSES — Those mental processes that one is unable to bring into one's consciousness.

VULNERABILITY — Openess to attack, injury.

WHOLISTIC — Holistic, i.e., of or pertaining to the "complete picture" , the quantum picture, the complete circuitry. Concerned with wholes or integrated systems rather than their parts. As opposed to "atomistic".

WISDOM — The second sfira and the first of the four phases. Knowledge of the final ends of all aspects of reality.

WORLD OF BOTZ — See "Botz". The everyday illusion "reality" of "uncertainty" and suffering.

YEHIDA — Highest level of the soul. Total oneness with the Light of the Lord.

YESOD — Sixth of the seven sfirot of which Joseph is the chariot. The Sfira through which is emanated all light to our world.

YOD — Smallest and yet most powerful letter of the Aleph Beth. The first and initial letter of the Tetragrammaton.

YOHAI, RABBI SHIMON BAR — The Master Kabbalist and author of the Zohar, the foremost work of kabbalistic knowledge. For him, the limitations of time, space and motion simply did not exist.

ZADDIK — Righteous. Associated with the sfira of Yesod and the covenant.

ZOHAR — The basic source of the Kabbalah. Written by Rabbi Shimon bar Yohai while hiding from the Romans in a cave in Pe'quin for 13 years. Later brought to light by Rabbi Moses de Leon in Spain.

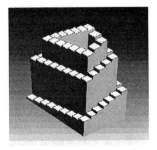

REFERENCES

1. Matan Torah, Y. Ashlag, Research Centre of Kabbalah, 1982, p.32.
2. Zohar Hadash, p.33a.
3. Exodus 20:5.
4. Ibid. 20:5.
5. Gates of Reincarnation, p.13.
6. Isaiah 6:7.
7. Zohar II, p.2b.
8. Isaiah 41:20.
9. Berg, Kabbalah for the Layman, Vol.I, p.112,125.
10. Ibid., p.13.
11. The Kirilian Reporter, p.9.
12. Oshtrand and Schroder, Behind the Iron Curtain.
13. Reach of the Mind, 1947.
14. Ten Luminous Emanations, vol. II, Berg, RCK, p.119.
15. Exodus 20:5.
16. Ibid., 20:4,5.
17. Gates of Reincarnation, p.32.
18. Gates of Reincarnation, p.58.
19. Ibid., p.59.
20. Ibid., p.186.
21. Kabbalah for the Layman, vol. I, Berg, p.81.

22. Gates of Reincarnation, p.186-187.
23. Exodus 21:1.
24. Zohar II, p.94a.
25. Exodus 35:1.
26. Ibid., 12:37.
27. Zohar I, p.22a; Gates of Reincarnation, p.83,37.
28. Zohar I, p.127a.
29. Gates of Reincarnation, p.35b.
30. Ibid., p.35a.
31. Ibid., p.123.
32. Ibid., p.125.
33. Ten Luminous Emanations, vol. I, p.64.
34. Zohar I, p.18b.
35. Gates of Reincarnation, p.35.
36. Ibid., p.32-33.
37. Zohar II, p.97a.
38. Gates of Reincarnation, p.9.
39. Lekutei Torah, Kitvei Ari, Research Centre of Kabbalah, 1970, p.152.
40. Exodus 21:13.
41. Lekutei Torah, Kitvei Ari, Research Centre of Kabbalah, 1970 p.152.
42. Tractate Sanhedrin, Talmud Bavli.
43. Zohar I, p.93a.
44. Zohar II, p.99a.
45. Zohar I, p.127a.
46. Zohar II, p.35a.
47. Zohar II, p.98b.
48. Zohar I, p.3a.
49. Genesis 11:27.
50. Genesis 25:22-24.
51. Kabbalah for the Layman, vol. I, Berg, p.93.
52. Ibid., p.88-92.
53. Kabbalah for the Layman, vol. I, Berg, p.78-80.
54. Kabbalah Connection, Berg, p. 151-154.
55. Kabbalah for the Layman, vol. I, Berg, p19.
56. Kabbalah for the Layman, vol. I, Berg, p.101-104.
57. Sulan Arukh, Laws of Charity, Biur Hagra, 247a; Deuteronomy 15:10.
58. Ecclesiastes 11:1.
59. Leviticus 19:18.
60. Gates of Reincarnation, p. 27b.
61. Zohar Hadash, Song of Songs, p.70,sec. 3.
62. Ibid., p.70, sec.4.

63. Song of Songs 1:7.
64. Zohar Hadash, Song of Songs, p.70, sec.5.
65. Song of Songs 1:8.
66. Ibid., 1:8.
67. Zohar Hadash, Song of Songs, p.70, sec.4.
68. Numbers 20:8-11.
69. Avot, 2:5.
70. Ten Luminous Emanations, vol. I, p.32.
71. Zohar I, p.91a.
72. Gates of Reincarnation, p.37.
73. Ecclesiastes 1:9.
74. Zohar Hadash, Song of Songs, p.70, sec. 3.
75. Gates of Reincarnation, p.32.
76. Zohar II, p.106a.
77. Exodus 21:3.
78. Zohar I, p.92a.
79. Deuteronomy 24:1.
80. Zohar II, p.107b.
81. Gates of Reincarnation, p.83.
82. Genesis 1:28.
83. Ibid., 3:20.
84. Zohar I, p.37a.
85. Genesis 16:2.
86. Ibid., 24:60.
87. Ibid., 30:1.
88. Psalms, 128:3.
89. Zohar III, p.149b.
90. Genesis 38:1.
91. Shnei Lukhot HaBrit, Horovitz.
92. Genesis 1:6.
93. Zohar III, p.9b.
94. Kabbalah for the Layman, vol. I, Berg, p.107.
95. Zohar II, p.94a.
96. Gates of Reincarnation, p.54.
97. Kabbalah for the layman, vol. I, Berg, p.86-88.
98. Zohar III, p.109a.
99. Zohar II, p.7b.
100. Shulhan Arukh, Orakh Hayyim, ch. 143.
101. Genesis 11:1.
102. Zohar I, p.76a-76b.
103. Genesis 11:7-9.

104. Zohar I, p.238a.
105. Zohar I, p.37b.
106. Genesis 5:1.
107. Ibid., 5:22; Proverbs 22:6.
108. Psalms 25:14.
109. Zohar III, p.10a.
110. Plato, Timaeus.
111. Genesis 9:21.
112. Numbers 12:7.
113. Ezekiel 36:27.
114. Zohar I,p.75b.
115. Zephaniah 3:9.
116. Zohar I, p.117b.
117. Zohar III, p.124b.
118. Psalms 104:24-26.
119. Zohar III, p.10a.
120. Avot, p.4:14; Tractates Ber, 53b; Sanhedrin, p.20b.
121. Tractate Sanhedrin, p.97a.
122. Zohar II, p.7b.
123. Psalms 46:2-3.
124. Tractate Shabbat.
125. Genesis 19:1.
126. Zohar I,p.106b.
127. Ibid., p.105b.
128. Ibid., p.106b.
129. Genesis 23:17-18.
130. Zohar I, p.127a.
131. Ibid., p.128b.
132. Genesis 23:17.
133. Zohar III, p.68a,b.
134. Kabbalah for the Layman, vol. I, Berg, p.107,108.
135. Zohar III, p.43a and b.
136. Gates of Reincarnation, pp.136-150.
137. Zohar III, p.44b.
138. Hos. 11:10.
139. Deut. 24:1.
140. Zohar II, p.103a.
141. Ibid., p.101b, 102a.
142. Gates of Reincarnation, p.8.
143. Samuel II, 12:13.
144. Zohar I, p.73b.

145. Exodus 20:14.
146. Psalms 51:5.
147. Ibid.
148. Samuel II, 12:24.
149. Samuel II, 11:24.
150. Zohar II, p.107a.
151. Gates of Reincarnation, p.53.
152. Ibid.
153. Zohar I, p.41a.
154. Ibid., p.134b.
155. Kabbalah Connection, Berg, p.107.
156. Sefer Yetzirah, Jerusalem, ed. 1962,R. Mordecai Atiyah, p.119.
157. Ibid., p.116.
158. Gates of Reincarnation, p.33.
159. Zohar I, p.78a.
160. Kabbalah for the Layman, vol. I, Berg, p.88.
161. Ibid., p.177.
162. Ibid., p.101-103.

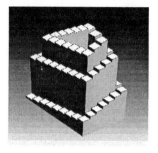

INDEX